"The Business Leaders Essential Guide to Marketing"

How to make sure your marketing delivers results

The reason your marketing might fail and how to fix it

Stephen Dann

Copyright ©2022 by Stephen Dann

All rights reserved. No part of this publication may be reproduced, distributed, or transmitted in any form or by any means without the permission of the author.

Published in the United Kingdom by Business Impact Solutions Ltd

Book design & layout by Velin@Perseus-Design.com

Email: bisbooks@businessimpactsolutions.co.uk
Website: www.businessimpactsolutions.co.uk

Paperback: 978-1-7399798-3-6

First Edition

The Business Leaders Essential Guide to Marketing

Marketing rarely seems to deliver on its promise.

You probably don't have the budgets to compete with the big players. You find it difficult to justify spending all that money and you cannot be sure if your marketing budget is being wasted. Maybe you've hired marketing managers, experts or agencies who have promised much, but achieved little.

Whatever your situation a practical detailed marketing plan with specific objectives, actions, and measures is essential - backed by a robust management process to keep the plan on track and ensure delivery.

Without these two essential components your marketing will be ineffectual, slow, and underwhelming and your investments destined for failure.

In *The Business Leaders Essential Guide to Marketing*, renowned business adviser, Stephen Dann sets out the methods, the tools, and the techniques to enable you to plan your marketing activity with clear measurable results and ensure you gain new customers.

Whether you are a business owner, marketer, or entrepreneur, *The Business Leaders Essential Guide to Marketing* enables you to develop and implement marketing plans to achieve your commercial goals.

You discover:

- Why marketing fails
- How to assess your current situation
- How to define your ideal customer
- How to develop messaging and brands
- Where to focus and what to measure
- What's in your marketing plan
- The process to ensure your marketing plans are implemented
- What might go wrong

Acknowledgements

I am fortunate to have begun my marketing career in the days before we had the amazing technology tools we have today. So, I have had a fantastic journey exploring and applying every wave of new technology to the marketing task. Along the way I have worked with so many innovative marketers dedicated to innovation, breaking new ground, constantly experimenting, and achieving astonishing results. There are too many to mention but thank you to everyone - you know who you are.

I have worked with some amazing teams; thank you for being curious, pushing the boundaries and being constantly willing to do things differently.

The ideas and processes in this book are drawn from and honed in real life experience - some of these approaches are original, others are adapted from more established practice. So, I'm grateful to those whose ideas I have built on, though I can't recognise you individually, and to the many clients who have trusted me to guide their marketing.

Finally thank you to Chris Bullick for writing the foreword. Chris is one of the rare examples of a pre-eminent marketer who has excelled on both sides of the client/agency fence, and I greatly appreciate his support with this project.

Foreword

When Stephen Dann asked me to suggest some marketing books for the Recommended Reading section of this book, I was shocked how short my list was. Is it because of marketing's mystical situation between science and art that there are so many fewer practical handbooks than there are for a discipline like say accounting?

This is especially true in terms of practical advice for the SME-based entrepreneur, owner or senior manager who manages a marketer but isn't one. How much marketing knowledge do you need to feel confident that your company and your marketing team are actually doing some useful marketing? As Stephen says in the book – not many people start a company in order to do marketing. (I guess I am the exception!)

As such, this book in Stephen's "Business Leaders Essential Guides" series fills an almost empty slot, and I can't think of anyone with better credentials to provide it. At Pull we help clients define their brands and market them. We do this for businesses typically in the

£10-£100m turnover bracket. What has stuck me throughout our journey is how the marketing press is almost entirely geared to the big FMCG brand audience. Consumer brands with mass market awareness and emblematic campaigns whose media budgets run into the tens of millions.

But what about smaller brands with low overall awareness but high potential? B2B brands? Brands who can't calculate their market share? A lot of what we do at Pull is translating the big brand's methodologies into workable approaches for smaller brands who need to be pragmatic and prudent with their cash but not use this as an excuse not to have a plan.

This book masterfully captures a wealth of these types of practical approaches. It provides a thorough but efficiently presented formula for the non-marketer who needs to make sure their company has complete and effective marketing plans, and measures their effectiveness.

It's also a great reference for those who do consider themselves the marketing experts too! I shall certainly keep my copy to hand.

Chris Bullick

Owner and Managing Director, The Pull Agency

Introduction

Marketing. The word seems to strike fear into the heart of many business owners.

You probably don't have the budgets to compete with the big players. You find it difficult to justify spending all that money and you cannot be sure if your marketing budget is being wasted. Maybe you've hired marketing managers, experts or agencies who have promised much, but achieved little.

Over many years I have asked entrepreneurs and business owners the same two questions. "What do you really enjoy doing in your business?" "What are the things that you really dislike doing?"

Whilst the things they like doing are many and varied and relate to the specific focus of each business. Consistently, nobody likes doing sales, and nobody likes marketing.

This is not surprising. You do not start a business to do sales or marketing. You start a business because you have a particular passion, skill, or talent. You believe that customers will appreciate it, demand it, and value it.

If you are an expert in sales and marketing, the chances are that you are doing that in someone else's business rather than your own. So, no one founds a business to do sales or marketing.

I have built and managed marketing teams in five major international organisations as well as consulting with over 400 organisations ranging from early-stage start-up right through to giant corporates. From this real-world experience, I have distilled a simple approach. This ensures you will never again question your investment in marketing, and you will achieve the results you require.

By the time you have read through this book you will be able to plan your marketing activity with clear measurable results and ensure you gain new customers. You should also be able to retain your existing customers and grow their revenue with you at the same time.

Table of Contents

The Business Leaders Essential Guide to Marketing 3
Acknowledgements 5
Foreword 7
Introduction 9
Table of Contents 11
1. Why Marketing Fails? 13
2. Where are you now? 17
3. What do you believe in? 33
4. What does your ideal customer look like? 39
5. How does it all fit together? 63
6. What's in it for your customers? 69
7. What do you want to say? 77
8. What are the marketing goals? 93
9. How are you going to achieve the goals? 101
10. What are the specific activities and tasks? 105
11. How are you going to schedule and ensure delivery? 111
12. How are you going to measure results? 121
13. What's in the plan? 131
14. What might go wrong? 137
15. Recommended Reading 143
About the Author 145

1.

Why Marketing Fails?

The reason: lack of a practical detailed marketing plan with specific objectives, actions, and measures. Coupled with the lack of a management process to keep the plan on track and ensure delivery.

Marketing is an investment, and like any investment should generate a return. Before making any investment, you would normally be clear on the expected return that you required, the outcome, the results, and the timescale. If you recruited a new salesperson, you would be clear on the sales target they were expected to achieve.

Your marketing investments are no different. Yet much marketing activity is based more on trust and hope which is more like gambling or playing the lottery. You might win big but mostly you will not.

The outcome of this is wasted money, and a continual cycle of replacement marketing people and agencies in the hope that the next iteration will come good. It does not have to be this way.

The other outcome is a reluctance to spend, and excessive stifling control. As a result, your marketing is underfunded, ineffectual, slow, and underwhelming.

You may well have come across some of the many marketing frameworks based on the letter "P" such as the 8 "Ps". (the original 4: Product, Place, Price and Promotion, with 4 extra "Ps" : People, Process, Physical Evidence & Partners).

Whilst we will touch on all these, the prime focus will rest on the 5 Ps: Proper Planning Prevents Poor Performance.

The rest of this book will focus on how to get this right.

Now is an exciting and challenging time to be a marketer. Today's marketer needs to be:

- as IT savvy as the IT team and as financially sharp as the Finance department
- a first-class project manager and a top rate data analyst
- a total expert on the sector and passionate about the product
- totally engaged with customers and guided by deep insight
- bang up to date on digital platforms, tools, and techniques
- supremely creative and a great communicator.

Successful future marketers must have mind-sets which are Innovative, Curious, Experimental, Fast, Responsive, Rigorous and Disciplined. Only committed marketing professionals need apply!

2.

Where are you now?

Let's start at the beginning.

The first thing we need to do is define the current situation. All marketers love doing Situation Analysis. This can seem an irritating and unnecessary procrastination when you want them to get down to the real stuff. But, unless there's a proper understanding of the base point you are working from, especially the current perceptions and behaviours of your customers, and the strengths and weaknesses of your current marketing practices, it's impossible to define a successful route forward.

However, marketers are sometimes guilty of failing to draw detailed adequate conclusions from the analysis which leads to future action. Analysis without conclusions and next steps is a worthless academic exercise.

Marketing Focus

So what is this plan focusing on? Is it a marketing plan for the whole business, a product range, an individual product, or brand? Do you want your marketing to target a specific geography or sector or type of customer?

A clear definition and description will help ground marketing thinking and activity into a specific context.

What is it and what does it do?

What is the history and the journey so far?

What has the journey been like so far?

How important is achieving marketing success?

What is your story's audience? What are their needs?

What does your audience think, feel, know, want?

Where are you now?

TELL YOUR STORY

WHAT IS IT THAT YOUR COMPANY OR PRODUCT DOES?

WHAT IS THE BACKGROUND OR HISTORY?

WHAT HAS THE JOURNEY BEEN LIKE SO FAR?

WHAT IS YOUR STORY'S AUDIENCE?

WHAT ARE THEIR NEEDS?

WHAT DOES YOUR AUDIENCE THINK, FEEL, KNOW, WANT?

OTSW not SWOT

Most SWOT analyses cover a wide range of facts, issues and opinions yet fail to provide any useful insight to help steer the direction for marketing. To be useful for marketing we need to narrow the focus and filter out irrelevant aspects. So, start by focussing on Opportunities.

A marketing focused SWOT analysis should be fully aligned with the nature of the opportunity which the marketing investment will be required to impact. By its very nature marketing thinking should be constantly focused on the external marketplace and the customers world, on the issues and concerns that occupy their minds.

So, starting with the external environment you should define the specific market opportunities which the business has identified for priority focus. The marketing team should have been deeply involved with identifying these opportunities, so there should be no surprises. These opportunities need to be defined in as much detail as possible. Try and avoid loose generalisations. At the end of the day, you want your marketing team to be able to apply laser focus onto these opportunities. Therefore, the more clearly, they are defined the better.

Next, list the external threats to the business. By definition, these are outside of your control. However, it is important to understand the risks and headwinds which might disrupt your plans. Threats can be summarised under headings such as Political, Economic,

Social, Technological, Environmental and Legal factors (PESTLE) but should not be restricted to this. Competitors deserve special attention, so we will be dealing with them separately.

Now consider the internal strengths of the business. In particular, the strengths of its marketing approach in relation to the specific opportunities. There may be strengths in other aspects but for this purpose only strengths that positively assist in developing the opportunity are relevant. You can go one stage further and only list strengths that a customer would recognise - since these are the factors which customers will use in their decision on whether to buy. Over belief in strengths which in reality have no impact, has led many businesses to believe they have an invincible position. Only to find that a new competitor sneaks in and steals their market by doing the one thing customers really care about, extremely well.

Similarly, with weaknesses, note down both business and marketing weaknesses. Again, only list those which will directly hold you back from fulfilling the opportunities, and which a customer would recognise, be aware of, and value.

OTSW

THE MARKET

EXTERNAL OPPORTUNITIES?	EXTERNAL THREATS?

THE BUSINESS AND ITS MARKETING

INTERNAL OPPORTUNITIES?	INTERNAL THREATS?

CUSTOMERS' PERCEPTIONS

YOUR STRENGTHS?	YOUR WEAKNESSES?

Business Environment Future Scan

Unfortunately, the world does not stand still. Since marketing is an investment which should have short, medium, and long-term impact, it is important to consider how the landscape might change in the future. Sound understanding of the foreseeable future will put you in a better position to cope with unexpected events.

Key Trends and Foresight
How will technology evolve?
What new technologies will emerge?
What existing technologies will become obsolete?
How will users embrace and use technology?

What trends are there in regulation?
Will new restrictions regulations and controls come into play?
Will these be favourable or unfavourable?

How will society and culture change and evolve?
Will this make your offering more, or less relevant?

What are the key Socioeconomic and demographic trends?
How might these impact on customer behaviour and your offering?

Market forecast
How will your key Market segments change and evolve?

Will their needs and demands in the future be different to today?

What new issues and challenges will your customers face?

Will it become easier for them to switch to alternative suppliers?

Will changes in the market make your current customers more, or less attractive?

Which customer segments are growing, which are declining?

Economic forecast
What is the state of the economy? Is the trend upwards downwards or flat?

What is the state of the global economy, and the major economic forces between major countries?

How easy is it to get investment and funding?

What is the impact for availability of raw materials or components?

What are the trends in employment and availability of talent?

Industry and sector analysis
How might your key competitors evolve and become stronger or weaker?

How might new players enter the market or small players become disruptive?

What new products might become a substitute or replacement?

What else might change or influence your sector?

What are the key drivers for innovation in the sector?

"The Business Leaders Essential Guide to Marketing"

FUTURE SCAN

HOW MIGHT THE LANDSCAPE CHANGE IN THE FUTURE? SHORT, MEDIUM, OR LONG TERM?

KEY TRENDS AND FORESIGHT
TECHNOLOGY, REGULATORY, SOCIETY & CULTURE, SOCIOECONOMIC

MARKET FORECAST
MARKET SEGMENTS, NEEDS & DEMANDS, MARKET ISSUES, SWITCHING COSTS, REVENUE ATTRACTIVENESS, MARKET ANALYSIS

ECONOMIC FORECAST
ECONOMIC INFRASTRUCTURE, COMMODITIES & RESOURCES, CAPITAL MARKETS, GLOBAL MARKET CONDITIONS

INDUSTRY AND SECTOR ANALYSIS
SUPPLIERS & OTHER ACTORS, STAKEHOLDERS, COMPETITORS, NEW ENTRANTS, SUBSTITUTE PRODUCTS OR SERVICES

Competitors

Everyone of your customers is also your competitors' prospect. If your marketing plan is to drive growth and increase sales, then unless your product or service is completely new and unique you will be needing to persuade your competitors' customers to switch to you. So, it is always crucial to maintain a full understanding of your key direct competitors and to monitor their marketing activity.

So, we need to list the strengths and weaknesses of each competitors offer and offering, as well as detailing their current marketing practises. What tools and techniques are they using? What sort of promotions? What key messages? Are they targeting specific segments?

Start with auditing your competitor's website, checking the content, style tone and messages, plus any news items or updates. Digital activity is very visible so it should be easy to keep an eye on their digital campaigns and social media.

If you want to go further, you can commission specific market research or mystery shopping.

Every time you lose a customer or fail to win an order, always ask where they have gone to and why?

(Tip: as you monitor your competitors keep a log of ideas of what they are doing which you may be able to emulate or improve on.)

You will also have indirect competitors who are competing for the same customer budget. So do not neglect the wider choices and options that your customers can consider. There are often many alternative ways to solve a problem and fulfil a need.

Finally, consider what your competitor would need to do to obstruct your marketing? For example, they may have huge budgets and can outbid you for advertising space or key brand terms.

COMPETITORS

WHO ARE YOU UP AGAINST?
THESE CAN BE SPECIFIC COMPANIES, PRODUCTS, OR CATEGORIES OF COMPETITOR AS WELL AS ALTERNATIVE WAYS THAT CLIENTS HAVE OF FULFILLING THE NEED:

WHO/WHAT?	THEIR STRENGTHS?	THEIR WEAKNESSES?	ABILITY TO HURT YOU?

Conversion model

What is your current conversion model across all channels and media at each stage of the customer journey?

How many clicks, or visitors, or impressions, or form completions, or calls, or enquiries or sales visits does it take to get a new customer? What does it cost at each stage and what is the timeline?

This basic model should cover new customer acquisition and existing customer retention metrics.

You may start your plan thinking you need more leads but focussing on improving the conversion rate is a much better place to start. Most websites do not suffer from having insufficient traffic, but from either failing to convert their traffic or attracting the wrong visitors.

Key Issues

So, from all the above, what are the key issues, problems and challenges you need your marketing to address?

Is it simply to generate more new business leads? or is it to raise awareness on an ongoing basis through social media? or to fight head-to-head with a competitor? Or launch a new product?

As always it is not possible to do everything. So, it is crucial that from the situation analysis your marketing team has real clarity on what are the core areas they must focus on. A plan which tries to do everything, is destined to fail.

KEY ISSUES

WHAT ARE THE CONCLUSIONS FROM THE SITUATION ANALYSIS?

3.

What do you believe in?

A clearly defined company or brand purpose is an essential anchor point for marketing. Defining purpose is comparatively easy for some organisations where they are aligned to a specific cause such as disease or suffering. In these situations, the purpose is abundantly clear.

For most organisations this is a much more difficult exercise.

Ask yourself what would happen if your product or service was banned so that no one could buy it anymore. How would your customers feel? What emotions would this trigger in them? Would they care? If the answer is, "they would just shrug and go and buy something else" then we have some work to do!

We explored purpose from the overall company perspective in the first book in this series (The Business Leaders Essential Guide to Growth). Businesses with purpose grow faster and retain staff better, but how does this roll out into marketing?

Modern marketing requires authenticity. With the ready availability of information and opinion through digital media, review platforms and social media channels, marketers cannot get away with fabrication, shades of grey or half-truths. Simply slapping on a coat of "purpose wash" to appear more relevant will not do. Customers will see through it and expose it. Apart from which, it is far easier to be straight forward, honest, and truthful.

Ultimately customers want more than an excellent product. In most cases they are faced with a choice between many other excellent products available from your competitors. Simon Sinek in his famous TED talk on company purpose in 2010 taught us that "people don't buy what you do, they buy why you do it".

Why?

Why does the company or product or service exist? Why do you do what you do? What is the purpose of your company? What are you passionate about? In what ways do you make a difference? What do you really believe in or care about? Why would customers care if they could no longer buy your product?

How?

How do you do what you do for your customers? How is this unique?

What?

What are the specific things you do for your customers? What do they achieve from this? What impact does this have on them?

Results?

What benefits or outcomes do you receive as a result?

Overall, what are the guiding principles which will ensure your teams always perform at their best, work smoothly together, and deliver outstanding service to customers who will then enthusiastically reorder, endorse and recommend?

In general, we prefer to buy things from people we know, like, and trust - people who embrace and reflect our own values and principles. When was the last time you bought something from someone you did not like? (or went back a second time).

And here we come into one of the fundamental challenges for marketing - you cannot appeal to everyone. It is essential to narrow down your focus to a much more specific audience.

This makes it much easier to craft messages, write content and develop campaigns. It also ensures far greater impact can be achieved, than by spreading budget thinly. Not even the biggest companies in the world have a marketing budget big enough to reach everyone. There are also very few occasions where it is possible to define a purpose which is both genuine and appeals to everyone.

Setting out exactly your Why, How and What will translate into your marketing messages, customer language, website, content, and social media. It provides a clear filter for all marketing activity – if it does not align with your Why (and your How) you do not do it.

What do you believe in?

PURPOSE PYRAMID

MARKETING TEAM PERSPECTIVE

CUSTOMERS PERSPECTIVE

WHY?
(PASSION & BELIEF)

THIS IS 120% GENUINE.
I CAN BUILD CREATIVE AND IMPACTFUL MARKETING PROGRAMMES

IS IT AUTHENTIC? BELIEVABLE?
ALIGNED TO MY VALUES?

HOW?
(THE WAY WORK IS DONE)

I CAN APPLY ALL MY MARKETING SKILLS, INSIGHTS AND LEARN CONSTANTLY

IS IT UNIQUE?
DIFFERENT IN WAYS THAT MATTER TO ME?

WHAT?
(ESSENTIAL ACTIVITIES)

I CAN MEASURE MARKETING PERFORMANCE AND PREDICT RESULTS, TAKING PROMPT ACTION TO KEEP ON TRACK

WHAT IS THE IMPACT?
IS MY EXPERIENCE CONSISTENT THROUGHOUT?

RESULT?
(BENEFITS & OUTCOMES)

I'M PROUD TO BE PART OF THIS COMPANY & ENJOY TIME WITH MY COLLEAGUES. MY MARKETING SKILLS KEEP GROWING AND ARE RECOGNISED.

IS THE OUTCOME / BENEFIT AS GOOD AS EXPECTED? I'LL TELL MY FRIENDS AND FAMILY ABOUT THIS

4.

What does your ideal customer look like?

The core foundation for all marketing is the customer. Really having deep insight, focus and knowledge of the people who will be choosing to buy your product or use your service. It makes no difference whether you are focusing on business to business, or business to consumer. At all times, the decision is being taken by an individual or individuals. Without a deep understanding of their audience, marketers cannot ensure the product, service, offering, messages, resources, communications, and campaigns will be successful.

Customer Profiles

To achieve this, for each category of customer you will need to develop a clear factual profile, understand their personality, their needs, wants and behaviours. Armed with this information you will be able to ensure your marketing is focussed for best effect. You'll be able to proactively seek out potential customers with the same profile.

The best place to start to identify what your ideal customer looks like is in your own customer database. Consider which of your current customers have the characteristics of being ideal for your business. This may be a combination of their commercial value and their behaviour or loyalty. The most productive place to target your marketing will be prospective customers with similar characteristics and profile. (Tip: Always monitor who your best customers are and how they found you.)

What are their demographic characteristics?

How old are they?
Are they male or female?

What sort of level of income do they have?
Do they live on their own?
Do they work? In what sort of job?

If you are a business-to-business marketer, you would want to understand: the Industry Sector, Company Size, Job Role, Job Function and Seniority. You would also need to understand their impact on the decision-making process. Are they primarily an influencer, an implementer, the user, or decision maker?

Are there any geographic factors or specific areas with hotspots of customers, gaps, or new territories to be explored?

To complete the target customer profile, list the Key Issues, Challenges, Problems, Opportunities for each group of customers. This should be factual information not supposition or opinion:

> What is their key challenge or problem?
> What is the pain for them because of this?
> What are the financial consequences this causes?
> What is the one key feature and one key benefit you offer which solves their problem?
> What is the impact that using your product or service gives them?

Further on in this book when we consider marketing tactics, one route may be to acquire databases for direct marketing purposes. The target customer profile provides the template for sourcing data.

TARGET CUSTOMER PROFILE

- INDUSTRY SECTOR
- COMPANY SIZE
- JOB ROLE / FUNCTION / SENIORITY
- GEOGRAPHY
- DEMOGRAPHY
- ISSUES, CHALLENGES, PROBLEMS, OPPORTUNITIES

A) WHAT IS THEIR KEY CHALLENGE OR PROBLEM?

B) WHAT IS THE PAIN FOR THEM AS A RESULT OF THIS?

C) WHAT ARE THE FINANCIAL CONSEQUENCES THIS CAUSES?

D) WHAT IS THE ONE KEY BENEFIT OF YOUR SERVICE WHICH SOLVES THEIR PROBLEM?

E) WHAT IS THE IMPACT THAT USING YOUR PRODUCT OR SERVICE GIVES THEM?

Customer Personas

Now we can move on to develop a more in-depth persona or avatar. The persona extends the information in the profile to provide a much fuller picture of the person you are trying to reach and influence. It includes their characteristics, motivation, personality, lifestyle, values, and behaviours.

Unfortunately, some marketers are tempted to construct detailed customer personas which are based more on their own perceptions rather than soundly researched reality. Simply running a brainstorm session to create personas is not sufficient. So always root the creation of personas in real life interviews with customers to eliminate self-reference bias.

It can be helpful to give each of your personas a personal name and photo. This brings them to life and becomes an easy shorthand to explain who you are targeting.

Here are some areas to include:

- Personal background and demographics
  Gender, age, family, household income, location, education, hobbies, interests.

- Professional background
  Employment, role, job title, company, career, knowledge, experience, skills, technologies, tools, qualifications, success measures, day in the life.

- Goals
  Aims, goals, ambitions, wants.

- Challenges
  Biggest challenges and responsibilities.

- Learning and Information sources
  Blogs, magazines, associations, social networks, TV.

- How we help
  How you solve your persona's challenges and help achieve their personal goals and business goals.

- Quotations
  Include actual comments and quotations from customers. Key phrases, jargon, mannerisms.

- Objections
  Identify the most common objections your persona will raise during the sales process.

- Marketing messaging
  How should you describe your solution to your persona? Language, terminology, level of complexity or technicality, factual or emotional, humorous, or serious.

- Elevator pitch
  Simple and consistent description.

What does your ideal customer look like?

CUSTOMER PERSONA TEMPLATE

- **PERSONAL BACKGROUND AND DEMOGRAPHICS**
- **PROFESSIONAL BACKGROUND**
- **GOALS**
- **CHALLENGES**
- **LEARNING AND INFORMATION SOURCES**
- **HOW WE HELP**
- **QUOTATIONS & COMMENTS**
- **OBJECTIONS**
- **MARKETING MESSAGING**
- **ELEVATOR PITCH**

Trends

Of course, the world does not stand still so it is important to consider how future trends will impact on your personas. How would you envisage them responding to those changes, challenges, and opportunities? Every year each one of your customers becomes a year older and their mindset, needs and desires will change slightly. Equally, a new year class will enter your persona group with slightly different ideas and thoughts. Therefore, your personas must not stand still. They need to be refreshed regularly to take into account the dynamic nature of the population and the world around us.

(Tip: Monitor the average age of customers. If it keeps increasing it means you are appealing to an aging customer base with the risk that your business may die out as they cease to be commercially active.)

Trigger Points

Customers do not exist in a constant state of need. So, even the best fit prospect will not be receptive to your messages and offerings at all times. In most situations the desire to buy is triggered by a particular event or set of circumstances. So, for each of your personas you must understand what it is that triggers the need for your product or service. What is it that creates the problem, situation or desire that suddenly motivates your persona to begin the process that leads to a purchase? The trigger point is the start of the process which, as we will see later, may take place over many months, many hours or just a few minutes before the customer buys.

Customer Journey Maps

This is one of those simple concepts that is actually quite difficult.

On their way to make a purchase, a customer goes through several different stages, experiences, and actions. Ideally you want to provide the customer with a smooth, positive, and frictionless experience. Your goal is to make it as easy as possible for them to understand your offering, appreciate its value, and place an order.

Most marketers will be familiar with the traditional AIDA model of the stages and steps a customer goes through whilst purchasing a product.

Attention – aware of a category, product, or brand

Interest – interested to learn about benefits

Desire – develops a positive view of the product

Action – begins purchase, checks prices / alternatives, tests, or makes a purchase

But in today's multi-channel information rich world we need to map this out in much more detail.

Once a customer realises they have a problem which they wish to solve, or a need to satisfy or a desire to fulfil; a whole sequence of activities and events take place which eventually end with a purchase. The customer journey map sets out the key stages the prospective customer goes through to engage with your product or service. We need to understand what people experience at every stage of the journey from first becoming aware, to placing the order and using the product or service. There will be touchpoints with the business which you can control and external influences which you cannot control directly.

The map is often drawn as a flow diagram so that each stage is clearly identified highlighting what the customer is trying to achieve and how you are fulfilling that to enable them to move on to the next step.

The customer journey is typically shown as a straightforward linear process which is a great place to start. However, the reality is that there will be multiple strands to the journey with many other influences beyond your control impacting on their decision. The other challenge is that customer behaviour varies constantly and may not follow exactly the same pattern every time.

For example, if you wish to buy a new sofa there would have been a phase in which you formed the view that your old sofa needs to be replaced. You may have searched online for sofas, seen someone else's sofa, and discussed it with friends and family. Then suddenly you begin to notice adverts for sofas and gradually educate yourself on all things "sofa". You are now a sofa expert and will quite likely know more about the specific type of sofa you want than any sofa sales assistant could. You have a good idea about what you like and do not like and will probably have formed a favourable or unfavourable view of particular brands. Now here is where it starts to get a bit random; you may happen to be walking through a shopping centre, pass the sofa store and call in. Or you might be searching online for something else, spot an advert and click on it. Or you might just type the sofa store in a search engine. The behaviour is driven by situation and circumstance not habit. When it comes to actually placing the order you might choose to do it face to face, online, or by phone. If you happen to need another sofa next week you may well order it differently. Especially if some aspect of your recent sofa buying experience has been good or bad.

So, the journey may not follow the same routes every time, even though the destination is the same. If the context is different, the behaviour may be different too.

Pirates and Funnels

The customer journey can be visualised in the form of a funnel with different content and communications aligned as the prospect moves towards a decision to buy. This will change depending on whether they are at the top, middle or bottom of the funnel.

In many situations today, the customer can become fully informed about your product or service long before you become aware of them. So, in the customer journey it is important to draw a distinction based on the stage in the journey at which you are engaging with people. If the customer has already researched and decided that yours is the brand they want, then it is counterproductive to send them content relevant to the early stage of a journey. Do not send "top of the funnel" content to customers who have already progressed to "bottom of the funnel".

For this example, we will use The Pirate Metrics (AARRR). (Tip: At each stage establish appropriate measures or metrics)

Acquisition
How do prospective customers first become interested and aware of your product or service.

Activation
How do they gain a deeper understanding of your product or service or experience it to enable them to seriously consider its value.

Retention
How many continue to engage with you and actively consider completing a purchase.

Revenue
How many place an order and become customers.

Referral
How many customers become genuine advocates and recommend your products to others.

At each stage prospects fall out of the funnel. So that not every prospect becomes a customer and not every customer is sufficiently delighted to recommend. It can be valuable to understand what happens to those potential customers who do fall out of the funnel and do not convert. Have they in fact continued and purchased from a competitor? Was there something that you could have done at that stage in their journey to service their needs better and to make it easier for them to select you?

"The Business Leaders Essential Guide to Marketing"

PIRATE METRICS

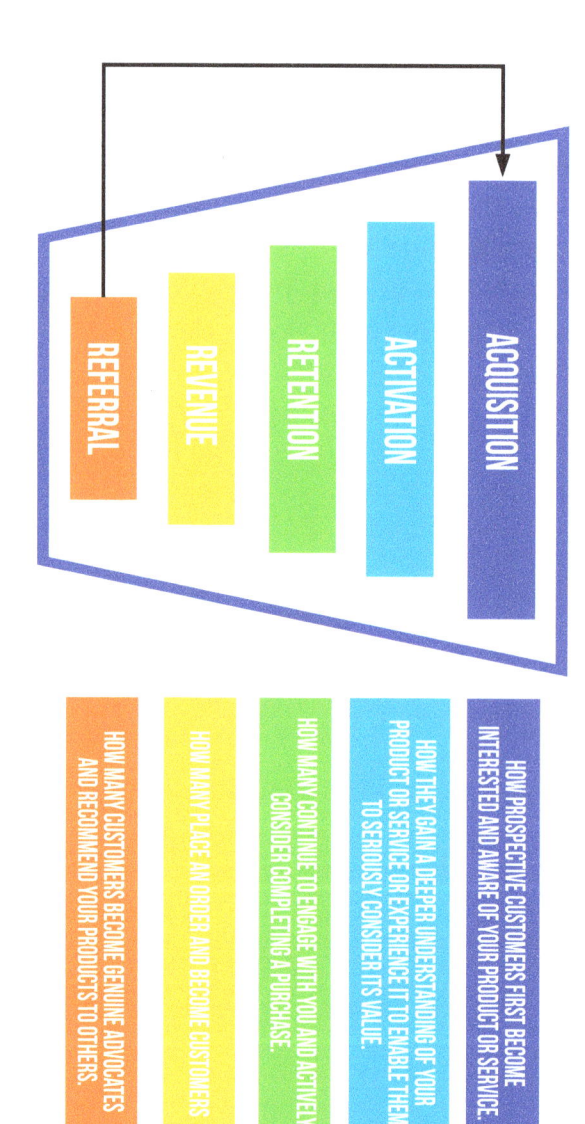

- **ACQUISITION** — HOW PROSPECTIVE CUSTOMERS FIRST BECOME INTERESTED AND AWARE OF YOUR PRODUCT OR SERVICE.
- **ACTIVATION** — HOW THEY GAIN A DEEPER UNDERSTANDING OF YOUR PRODUCT OR SERVICE OR EXPERIENCE IT TO ENABLE THEM TO SERIOUSLY CONSIDER ITS VALUE.
- **RETENTION** — HOW MANY CONTINUE TO ENGAGE WITH YOU AND ACTIVELY CONSIDER COMPLETING A PURCHASE.
- **REVENUE** — HOW MANY PLACE AN ORDER AND BECOME CUSTOMERS.
- **REFERRAL** — HOW MANY CUSTOMERS BECOME GENUINE ADVOCATES AND RECOMMEND YOUR PRODUCTS TO OTHERS.

Moments of truth

In any customer journey there are critical points at which the customer reaches a clear understanding or a moment of truth. There are usually several of these along the journey which need to be fulfilled at the right time for each. It is not possible just to present a single complete document that answers all of these at the same time. Moments of truth are the potential deal breakers.

The customer may have specific criteria that have to be met and need to understand how your product fits with their existing solutions. Then, they want to check approximate cost (not a quote) to establish if your solution is within the realms of possibility. From all this they would be able to confirm that the solution would work for them.

They might then follow a process to gain independent validation. They may talk to other people, check social media, or read reviews before coming back to discuss the price again. In business-to-business marketing, it is often at this point that you realise the "hot prospect" who you have nurtured so carefully, now has to gain approval from someone else.

So, there is now a whole new journey to map out in the customer's decision-making team.

Remember that in B2B, there is often a lot at stake personally for the individual who makes the decision if it does not work out. It is tempting to assume that B2B buyers will be purely focussed on business benefits, functionality, technical performance, and cost. However, the prime motivations are likely to be more personal: fun, pride, keep my job, easier life, make me look good, work life balance, promotion. Somewhere in this mix, "achieving business results" is a factor.

What does your ideal customer look like?

MOMENTS OF TRUTH

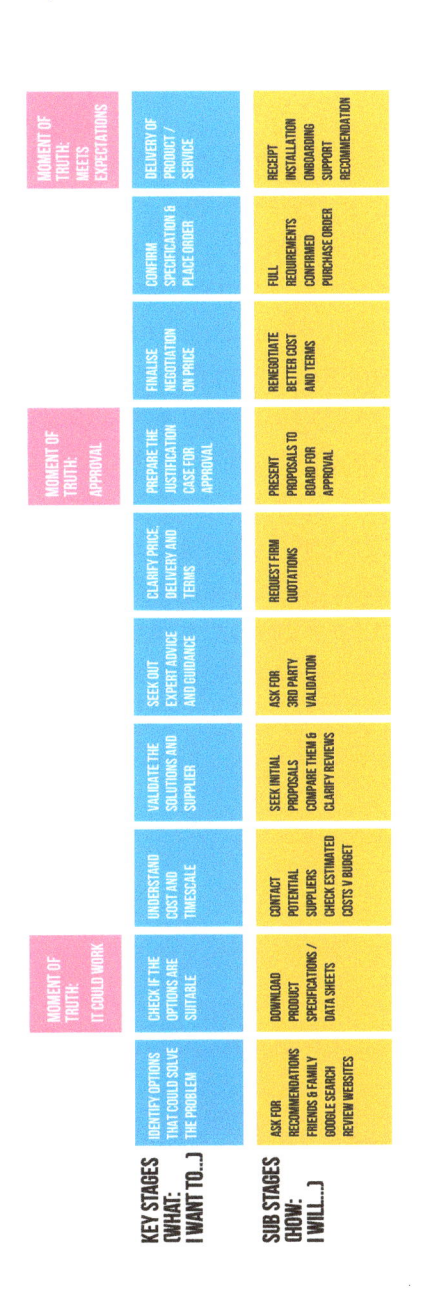

KEY STAGES (WHAT: I WANT TO...)	SUB STAGES (HOW: I WILL...)
MOMENT OF TRUTH: IT COULD WORK	
CHECK IF THE OPTIONS ARE SUITABLE	DOWNLOAD PRODUCT SPECIFICATIONS / DATA SHEETS
IDENTIFY OPTIONS THAT COULD SOLVE THE PROBLEM	ASK FOR RECOMMENDATIONS FRIENDS & FAMILY GOOGLE SEARCH REVIEW WEBSITES
UNDERSTAND COST AND TIMESCALE	CONTACT POTENTIAL SUPPLIERS CHECK ESTIMATED COSTS V BUDGET
VALIDATE THE SOLUTIONS AND SUPPLIER	SEEK INITIAL PROPOSALS COMPARE THEM & CLARIFY REVIEWS
SEEK OUT EXPERT ADVICE AND GUIDANCE	ASK FOR 3RD PARTY VALIDATION
CLARIFY PRICE, DELIVERY AND TERMS	REQUEST FIRM QUOTATIONS
MOMENT OF TRUTH: APPROVAL	
PREPARE THE JUSTIFICATION CASE FOR APPROVAL	PRESENT PROPOSALS TO BOARD FOR APPROVAL
FINALISE NEGOTIATION ON PRICE	RENEGOTIATE BETTER COST AND TERMS
CONFIRM SPECIFICATION & PLACE ORDER	FULL REQUIREMENTS CONFIRMED PURCHASE ORDER
MOMENT OF TRUTH: MEETS EXPECTATIONS	
DELIVERY OF PRODUCT / SERVICE	RECEIPT INSTALLATION ONBOARDING SUPPORT RECOMMENDATION

TIMESCALE

Customer Sentiment Mapping

Emotion plays a big part in purchase decisions. Throughout the customer journey, feelings and emotions can vary enormously from positive to negative - sometimes leading customers to abandon the process part way through. This can happen during a website transaction where customers may abandon the shopping cart before completing even if they do actually want the product. Maybe the site ran slow, or you asked one too many questions, or you pushed one too many offers, or some other minor factor which was sufficient to change the customer's mood from positive to negative. The customer may have a set of existing preconceptions about your product which will influence their receptiveness. So, at each stage of your customer journey establish how positive or negative their feelings are. Your coffee may be the best tasting in town, but having been drawn in by the aroma, if the queue is too long and I cannot find a seat, I will probably go elsewhere.

What does your ideal customer look like?

COFFEE SHOP SENTIMENTS

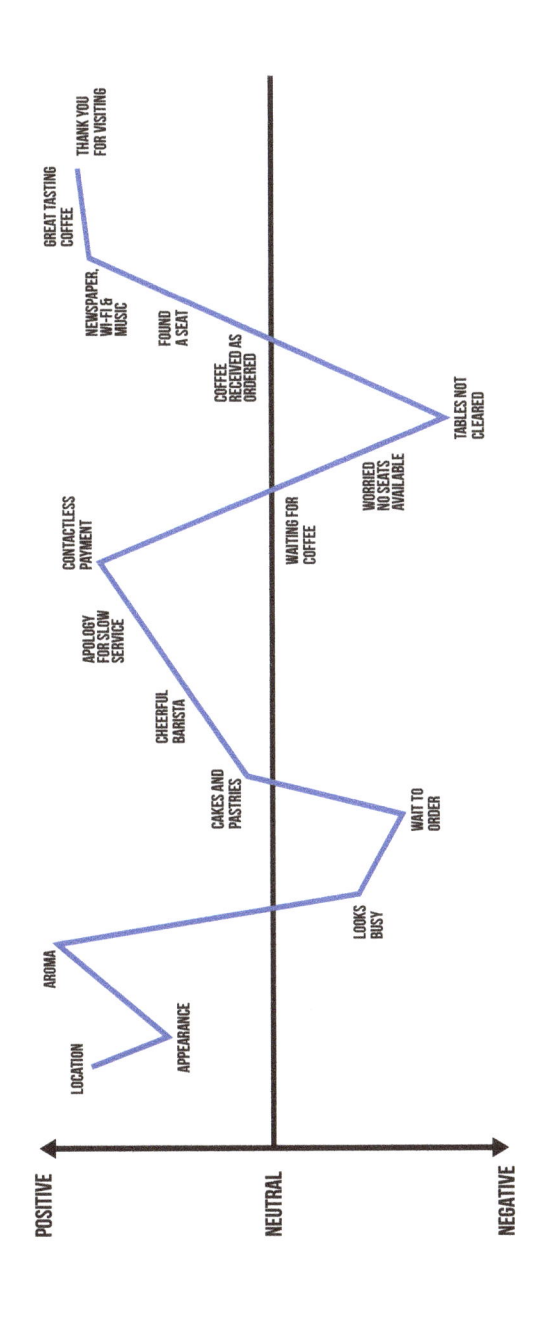

POSITIVE / NEUTRAL / NEGATIVE

- LOCATION
- APPEARANCE
- AROMA
- LOOKS BUSY
- WAIT TO ORDER
- CAKES AND PASTRIES
- CHEERFUL BARISTA
- APOLOGY FOR SLOW SERVICE
- CONTACTLESS PAYMENT
- WAITING FOR COFFEE
- WORRIED NO SEATS AVAILABLE
- TABLES NOT CLEARED
- COFFEE RECEIVED AS ORDERED
- FOUND A SEAT
- NEWSPAPER, WI-FI & MUSIC
- GREAT TASTING COFFEE
- THANK YOU FOR VISITING

Customer Research

There is nothing more important for a marketer than understanding and researching customers. These are the people who you want to reach and influence so that you really must understand the way they behave. Only then can you appreciate all the ways the business can satisfy the full breadth of their requirements in their relationship with you and ensure that your campaigns are well founded. (Tip: Always find out how a new customer found you, so you can do more of it.)

If in doubt, ask:

Telephone your top 10 customers and ask them these three simple questions:

    a) What do we do for you?
    b) Why do you choose us?
    c) How did you find us in the first place?

Then write down the exact words that they use. You may be surprised that both the perceptions and language used by customers will be significantly different to those used inside the business. Customer decisions are primarily driven by emotion in both business to consumer and business to business marketing, so expect more emotional than rational language.

Net Promotor Score

NPS is one of the most widely used customer satisfaction measures and benchmarks. It enables you to identify customers who are "detractors", "passive" or "promoters" of your product or brand.

The Net Promoter Score question is really simple:

"On a scale from 0 to 10, how likely are you to recommend our product / service to your friends, family or colleagues?"

A score of:

0 to 6 is a "detractor" – an unhappy customer who will spread negative comments

7 or 8 is "passive" – neutral, not fussed either way

9 or 10 is a "Promotor" – loyal, enthusiastic ambassadors and advocates

The NPS score is calculated by subtracting the percentage score of "promoters" from the "detractors" to provide a benchmark.

Understanding who your "promoters" are will provide a clear focus for marketing activities further on in the plan. But it is also essential to keep track of the Net Promotor Score over time to support activities that are improving it or to plan corrective action.

The benchmark can be used to compare with similar organisations in your sector but be careful not turn NPS in a vanity metric.

NPS

"ON A SCALE FROM 0 TO 10, HOW LIKELY ARE YOU TO RECOMMEND OUR PRODUCT / SERVICE TO YOUR FRIENDS, FAMILY OR COLLEAGUES?"

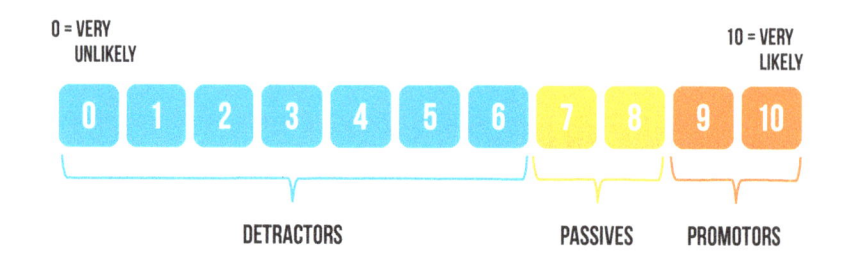

0 = VERY UNLIKELY

10 = VERY LIKELY

| 0 | 1 | 2 | 3 | 4 | 5 | 6 | 7 | 8 | 9 | 10 |

DETRACTORS (0–6)   PASSIVES (7–8)   PROMOTERS (9–10)

NPS = % OF PROMOTERS - % OF DETRACTORS

You should always ask the supplementary question "Why did you give us that score?" to improve understanding of the customer experience.

However, NPS should not be used in isolation, and should be viewed alongside wider customer research to ensure robust and balanced insight. By narrowing everything down to just one measure you may end up trying to improve the wrong thing and miss the wider opportunity to understand behaviour.

It is rare for customers to be able to accurately describe the true process and factors that influence their behaviour. Behaviour patterns often deviate from established models and thinking, sometimes driven by random factors, the context, or new influences. Customers are all individuals – a few will make snap decisions to buy, most need time to consider and some will never decide until circumstances force them to. So do not neglect the importance of intuition and insight alongside research and analysis.

(Tip: regularly sit in with your customer service team or call centre and listen in to what customers are saying, how they say it and what really matters.)

Know, Like, Trust

The communication and message clearly will evolve and change along the customer journey. If over time and with consistent messaging a customer knows you, likes you, and trusts you then they may proceed to buy from you. They will also recommend you to others.

5.

How does it all fit together?

The "Business Model" is the blueprint which defines how your business operates and makes money. The best way to visualise this is to use the Business Model Canvas created by Alexander Osterwalder and Yves Pigneur. The canvas sets out the 9 key parts to the business model covering Customers, Offering, Infrastructure and Financial Viability. These are all linked together so if something changes in one part of the model it affects some or all the others. The full Business Model Canvas was explored in the first book in this series (The Business Leaders Essential Guide to Growth). From a marketing perspective we need to focus on the Customers and Offerings which are on the right-hand side of the canvas:

Customer Segments

Who are you creating value for?

We need to be clear on what an ideal customer looks like so that the rest of the model can be aligned to serving their needs. You have already created detailed profiles and personas, but for this purpose, just use a brief overview of no more than four key segments you want to focus on. If you are in B2B, include industry sector, company size and job role of decision maker as well.

Value Proposition

What value do they receive?

This is all about what the customer gets out of the relationship. List the problems you are solving for customers, or the needs and wants you are satisfying. It is possible that different customer segments will require different value propositions or at least a different emphasis. They may be trying to resolve different problems, or the same problem in different ways. We will cover this in more detail in the next section.

Customer Relationships

How do you manage the relationship with your customers?

To deliver value to customers you must manage the relationship with them to achieve sales orders. Relationships may be face to face, virtual, online, telephone, email, via third parties. They may involve lengthy negotiations or just a click. Transactions could be one off or recurring.

Channels & Communications

How do you reach them?

Channels could be physical distribution channels to enable you to physically deliver products or channels of communication to enable you to deliver key messages and information to your chosen customer segments. What are the key marketing tools that you use to engage with customers?

Revenue Streams

What are the key revenue streams?

Your revenue can be categorised by customer segment, product or service line, geography or any other way that makes logical sense.

So, if the marketing goal is to increase the number of customers, this will be reflected by an increase in the revenue stream. The task is to decide which segments you are going to focus on to generate the extra revenue. If you already feel the segments are saturated, then there may be entirely new segments to be researched and understood. Either way, it is important to consider how the value that these new customers want may be different and therefore how the value proposition, message and focus might need to change. Will these new customers require changes in the way that you manage relationships? Will they need additional levels of support, guidance, training, or on-boarding? Which channels will you use to reach them? What are the key marketing tools it will be necessary to engage with them?

The Business Model Canvas also helps marketers map out the way to launch a new product by posing the same questions.

Who are you creating value for?

What is the value proposition?

How are you going to reach them?

How are you going to manage relationships with them?

What is the revenue forecast?

How does it all fit together?

BUSINESS MODEL CANVAS

BUSINESS / PRODUCT DESCRIPTION
- WHAT ARE WE FOCUSING ON?

KEY PARTNERS
- WHAT ACTIVITIES & RESOURCES ARE OUTSOURCED?

KEY ACTIVITIES
- WHAT ACTIVITIES ARE NEEDED TO DELIVER THE VALUE?

KEY RESOURCES
- WHAT RESOURCES DO YOU NEED TO DELIVER THE VALUE?

VALUE PROPOSITIONS
- WHAT VALUE DO THEY RECEIVE?

RELATIONSHIP MANAGEMENT
- HOW DO YOU MANAGE THE RELATIONSHIP?

DISTRIBUTION CHANNELS & COMMUNICATION
- HOW DO YOU REACH THEM?

CUSTOMER SEGMENTS
- WHO ARE YOU CREATING VALUE FOR?

COST STRUCTURE
- HOW MUCH DOES IT ALL COST?

REVENUE STREAMS
- WHAT ARE THE KEY REVENUE STREAMS?

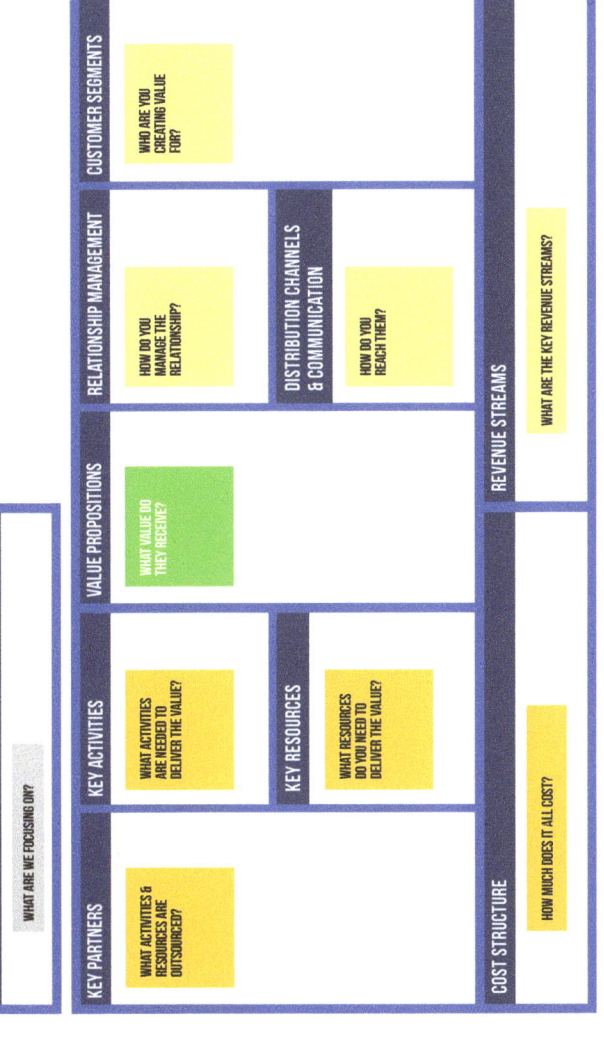

REF: "BUSINESS MODEL GENERATION" BY OSTERWALDER & PIGEUR

6.

What's in it for your customers?

Alongside the Customer, the Value Proposition is the essential foundation of marketing.

It brings together the understanding of customers' needs with how the product fulfils those needs. It describes the benefits which your product or service guarantees to deliver.

Customers are not really interested in your products or solutions, they are primarily interested in their own problems, challenges, and desires. Your value proposition must align with their agenda, which may also change through time, events, and experience.

Every business is based on satisfying customer needs and requirements by creating products and services which overcome their points of pain and create gains.

The Value Proposition provides a unifying focus for marketing by defining the:

- Value delivered
- Problem solved
- Product / Service offered
- Needs or wants satisfied

Customer's purpose

What are the tasks they are trying to perform or fulfil, the problems they are trying to solve, or the needs or wants they are trying to satisfy? When and how do these needs or wants occur? Customers may wish to avoid "pain" or obtain "gain", or both. They may be seeking benefits which are functional (solve a problem), external appearance (look good) or internal emotional (feel good). There will of course also be associated tasks which need to be satisfactorily fulfilled such as service and delivery which will form part of the customers need.

Customers Pains

What are the frustrations, fears, needs, negative emotions, undesired costs and situations, or risks that your customer experiences in trying to perform the tasks?

What worries them or keeps them awake at night?

What is stopping them from resolving the problem?

What is the overall negative situation they wish to escape from?

What are the associated tasks which discourage customers from completing a purchase for products they actually want?

Customers Gains

What benefits do your customers expect or desire?

What would surprise or delight them?

What additional functional utility, social gains, positive emotions, or cost savings do they want?

What would make their life easier, fulfil their dreams make them successful?

What is the overall positive impact they desire?

Products / Services

List all your products, services, or offerings which are relevant to the customer segment.

Consider which ones are most closely aligned with your customers pain and gain profiles, their wants, and needs. What are the associated tasks you perform in support of these offerings?

Pain Relievers

How do your products and services remove or alleviate customer pains?
Which of your customers pains do your products or services alleviate best?
How do they do this?

Gain Creators

How and how much do your products and services deliver customer gains.?
Which of your customers gains do your products or services achieve best?
How do they do this?

(Tip: The best way to visualise this is to use the Value Proposition Canvas created by Alexander Osterwalder and Yves Pigneur)

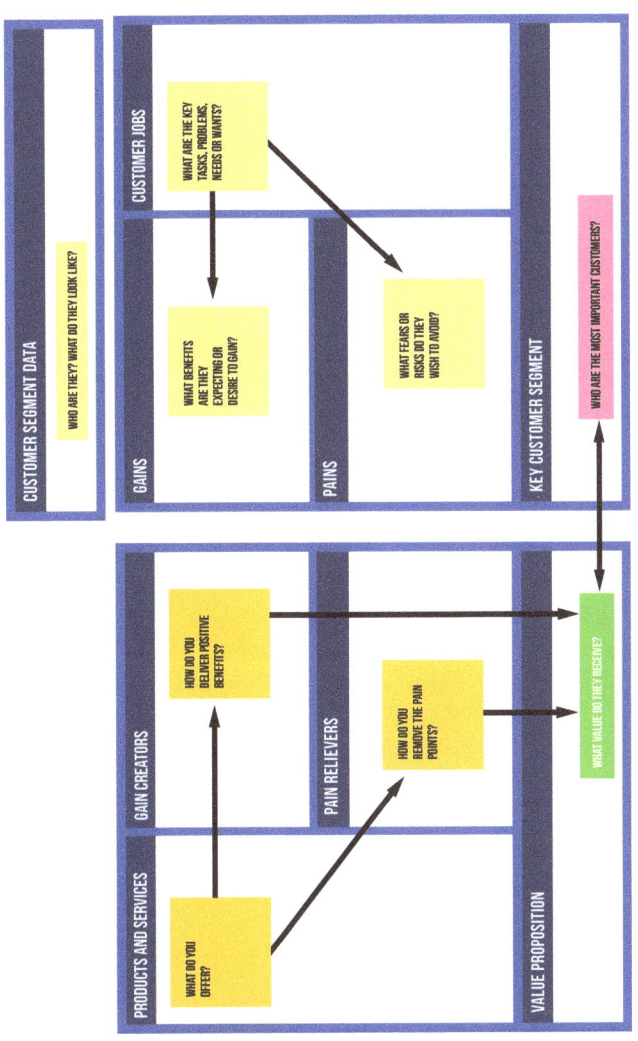

What's in it for your customers?

VALUE PROPOSITION CANVAS

CUSTOMER SEGMENT DATA
- Who are they? What do they look like?

CUSTOMER JOBS
- What are the key tasks, problems, needs or wants?

GAINS
- What benefits are they expecting or desire to gain?

PAINS
- What fears or risks do they wish to avoid?

KEY CUSTOMER SEGMENT
- Who are the most important customers?

PRODUCTS AND SERVICES
- What do you offer?

GAIN CREATORS
- How do you deliver positive benefits?

PAIN RELIEVERS
- How do you remove the pain points?

VALUE PROPOSITION
- What value do they receive?

REF: "VALUE PROPOSITION DESIGN", ALEXANDER OSTERWALDER, YVES PIGNEUR, GREG BERNARDA, AND ALAN SMITH

— 73 —

The value proposition should ideally focus on a single benefit which is the outcome for the customer. It should be specific, clear, and concise with a sense of urgency. It must mitigate your customers' pain or provide gain. The most compelling propositions focus on more emotional wants, rather than more functional needs.

Here are some frameworks to help refine your proposition:

What do you do or make?	
Who for?	
It solves what problem?	
With what benefits for your customer?	

To (Customer Persona) we are the (your role) that (helps) because we have (an attribute), Unlike (an alternative)

To …   We are the …   that …   because …   unlike …

Our products and services help (customer segment) who want (something done) by (doing something) and (doing something else), unlike (other solutions)

What's in it for your customers?

> We help…
> who want …
> by …
> and by …
> unlike …

Target Buying Incentive: "I will buy a product that (does something better) than any other product in the category"

Check your proposition

There are two fundamental aspects to check to make sure your proposition is valid. Your customers need to understand it and recognise it. And it needs to be different and distinct from your competitors.

For customers, simply ask some of your best customers what they think. Do they think this proposition is credible and would they recognise it as being your product or service? Does it reflect their own experience? Avoid using complicated online surveys as these will tend to produce skewed results. Nothing can beat face to face conversation with a real customer.

For competitors, review their websites, marketing campaigns, and sales collateral and dispassionately assess if the messaging is different. If you can simply remove their logo and replace it with your own, you need to go back to the drawing board. There is no point in promoting a value proposition which is identical or very similar to a competitor. Both search engines and potential customers will be unable to see the difference.

(Tip: create a word cloud of your competitors' websites and your own website, remove the company names, and see if your team can tell which is which)

7.

What do you want to say?

So, we now know who you are trying to reach. We know a lot about these particular types of customers, their interests, desires, and behaviours. We have established the specific products and services you will be offering to them. We understand the value they will receive from these products and how they will fulfil their problems, issues, challenges, needs, wants, and desires. Now we need to figure out how to construct the message to explain the proposition and tell your story.

Brands & Messaging

Whether you know it or not your company or product is a brand, the only question is whether you choose to manage it. A brand is made up of a collection of impressions, feelings, experiences, and emotions which a customer attributes to your product or company. Where these are all positive, customers will be drawn to your brand, seek it out and readily purchase. Where they are negative or neutral, they will be driven away and be open to your competitors offers. The brand map is a complex mix of experiences, communications and social proof which need to align consistently. Not all of these are in your control, however developing clear succinct and compelling messages are essential to gaining new customers.

In managing brand communications, there are many layers of message to consider. These need to be clearly defined to act as a reference point for content creation and campaigns so that the brand always talks with a consistent message and voice.

Content Audit

The starting point is to conduct a detailed audit of all the current content which describes, supports, or promotes your product. Check through the website, social media, sales collateral, presentations, PR, and advertisements. Across all of these, what is the current message, style, and tone, and how well does it align with your chosen personas?

(Tip: Word maps or word clouds are ideal ways of showing where the core focus and energy in existing content lies)

Brand Values

To establish the values for your product or brand, one way is to borrow values from un-associated products or brands in completely different sectors that may have similar characteristics. These should be the typical brands that your chosen personas favour, use or aspire to, not just brands that you like yourself. Always be careful not to self-reference and develop campaigns that appeal to you personally – you may not be the avatar for your customer.

Grab a notebook and write down the answers to the following:

What brand would your product, service or company be if you were a:

>   Car:
>   Supermarket:
>   Holiday destination:
>   Hotel chain:
>   Newspaper or news channel:
>   Drink:

What values do you associate with them?
Write down 3 adjectives (describing words) for each.

You will now have a list of potential brand values. A few may be inappropriate for your product or service so can be eliminated. Some will appear several times and will most likely be the core values for your brand.

BRAND VALUES

"WHAT WOULD YOUR COMPANY / PRODUCT BE IF IT WAS A ....?

	BRAND NAME	LIST 3 VALUES OR TERMS (ADJECTIVES) YOU ASSOCIATE WITH IT:
CAR		
HOTEL CHAIN		
WINE OR BEER		
SUPERMARKET		
NEWSPAPER OR NEWS CHANNEL		
HOLIDAY		

Brand Pyramid

Brand messages can be communicated at many different levels. It is crucial to understand how these fit together. This is often visualised as a Pyramid; starting with features at the bottom, working through the different layers to finish with brand essence at the top.

Features
These are the facts that state what your product or service is. In most cases there will be a list of features, many will be identical to those in competitors' products, but any unique features should be highlighted.

Functional benefits
These are the benefits which a customer receives from the features. The impact or outcome which you deliver at a functional level.

Emotional benefits
What is the emotional benefit? How does the customer now feel?

Values
What values underpin the way you deliver the functional and emotional benefits?

Essence
In just 3 or 4 words, what is the essence of your brand (Your "why")

What do you want to say?

BRAND PYRAMID

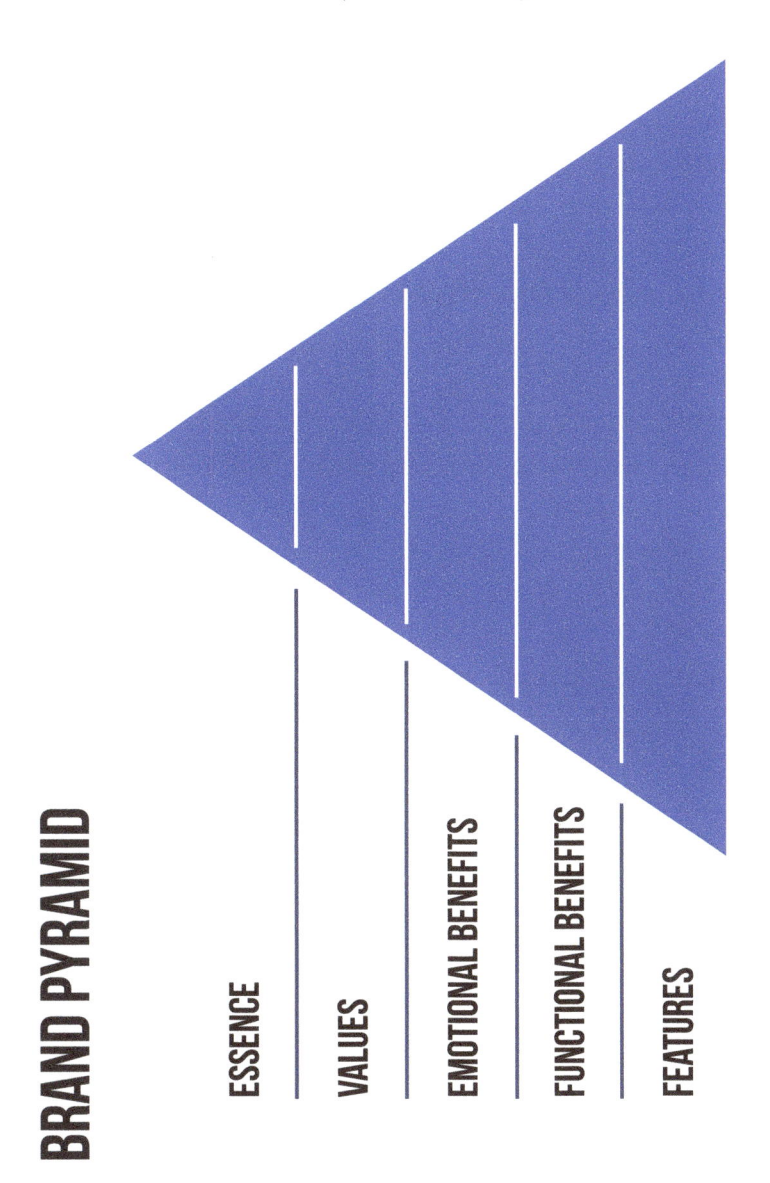

ESSENCE

VALUES

EMOTIONAL BENEFITS

FUNCTIONAL BENEFITS

FEATURES

It is easy for marketers to get lost in product features, after all every product is built and designed on its features. However, customers buy the benefits because it's the benefits that solve their problems or satisfy their needs and desires.

So, for example a firm of accountants might have this brand pyramid:

Features:
Audit, Risk Assurance, Tax Guidance, Bookkeeping, Financial Reporting, Compliance, Accounting, Business Valuations, Pensions Advice, Consulting

Functional benefits:
Compliance, Risk Management, Business Growth, Funding, Access to expertise, Best practice, Objective guidance, Knowledgebase

Emotional benefits:
Peace of mind, Confidence, Security, No surprises, Freedom to focus on what you do best

Values:
Honesty, Integrity, On your side, Relish your success

Essence:
Thrive, grow, prosper

There is a big shift in the message from features ("we do audits") to Essence ("we help you thrive, grow and prosper").

Brand Description
This is the simplest complete description of the brand. It should include key attributes and be distinct from other offerings. It defines what the product is and what it is not.

Brand Essence & Personality
What is the style and tone of voice for your brand?

Fun, Casual, Modern, Vibrant, Unique, Youthful, Quirky, Serious, Formal, Traditional, Muted, Familiar, Mature, Safe, Current, Desired?

As part of a rebrand process you may wish to change the style and tone, so define the before and after personality.

Brand Promise
What a brand delivers for its customers.

Brand Narrative
Stories are hugely compelling, so write down your brand's story. How did it start, what's happened over the years, what's changed, why does it exist and what next?

Elevator Pitch
You have 30 seconds in the elevator to persuade someone to buy. What would you say?

Hierarchy of message
All these messages fit together and provide a framework for marketing communications. At different times and situations,

you will need to talk at different levels. You now have a frame of reference to guide marketing activity, communicate the proposition, and always ensure consistency of message.

Case Study: Data Quality Software Company

The company is a world leader in data quality software and solutions, here is how the team redefined their brand and marketing messages:

Brand Pyramid:

Features:
Cleanse Data, Deduplication, Validation, Enrichment, Migrate, Integrate, Consult, Advise, Support, Custom development, Machine learning, Data audits, Data quality improvement.

Functional benefits:
Single Customer View, Control of data, Protection v Compliance (GDPR), Understand data, Customer Insight, Reduce cost / time, Less wastage, Improve customer experience, Reduce reputational risk, Better decisions.

Emotional benefits:
Confidence, Secure in role, Feel efficient, Buy in & support from users, Pride in work, Sense of worth (hero v villain)

Values:
Regain time, Enhance brand, Fulfil growth post change, Customer engagement / satisfaction, Efficiency

Essence:
Smooth, Efficient, Confident, Trustworthy

Brand Description:

"We provide a complete range of data management services to enable forward thinking managers to solve problems at every level and every stage of their data management journey…"

Brand Essence & Personality:

Reliable, high quality, established, technical, clean cut, trustworthy, personal, flexible, premium, good value and good values, adaptable, transparent, clear, get what you expect, fit for purpose, no surprises, individual, right balance of quality, customer experience, great service, helpful, informative, unbiased, straight to the point, up to date, value their views, authoritative, knowledgeable, expert, value for money, refreshing, efficiency.

Tone of voice

Clear, modern, unique, mature, professional, safe, pain reliever, helpful.

Brand Promise:

"We provide the foundations for data driven decisions to enable managers and teams to deliver projects & goals with confidence".

Brand Narrative:

"No one has been ensuring that data is fit for business for longer than us. Back in the 1990's in the heat of the dotcom boom, our founder identified that poor data quality was the number one bottleneck for the adoption of the emerging customer / contact management technologies. We have been at the forefront ever since. Today, we have the unique ability to solve any data problem thrown at us, so that clients can focus on delivering excellence to their customers. Those who work closely with us know the sense of relief and empowerment that comes from finally being liberated from data hell, with the ongoing security of first-class support whatever the issue, whenever it arises."

Elevator Pitch:

"We believe that everyone should have data they can trust. Clients tell us that they were frustrated with poor data quality which consistently exposed them to commercial risk and constraints on growth. So, we help people who are concerned with the quality of their data to ensure its clean and never gets dirty again".

"The Business Leaders Essential Guide to Marketing"

DATA QUALITY BRAND PYRAMID
"DRIVING DATA TRANSFORMATION"

ESSENCE
- SMOOTH
- EFFICIENT
- CONFIDENT
- TRUSTWORTHY

VALUES
- REGAIN TIME, ENHANCE BRAND, FULFIL GROWTH POST CHANGE, CUSTOMER ENGAGEMENT / SATISFACTION, EFFICIENCY

EMOTIONAL BENEFITS
- CONFIDENCE, SECURE IN ROLE, FEEL EFFICIENT, BUY IN & SUPPORT FROM USERS, PRIDE IN WORK, SENSE OF WORTH (HERO V VILLAIN)

FUNCTIONAL BENEFITS
- SINGLE CUSTOMER VIEW, CONTROL OF DATA, PROTECTION V COMPLIANCE (GDPR), UNDERSTAND DATA, CUSTOMER INSIGHT, REDUCE COST / TIME, LESS WASTAGE, IMPROVE CUSTOMER EXPERIENCE, REDUCE REPUTATIONAL RISK, BETTER DECISIONS

FEATURES
- CLEANSE DATA, DEDUPLICATION, VALIDATION, ENRICHMENT, MIGRATE, INTEGRATE, CONSULT, ADVISE, SUPPORT, CUSTOM DEVELOPMENT, MACHINE LEARNING, DATA AUDITS, DATA QUALITY IMPROVEMENT

What do you want to say?

Having completed this process, you will have a set of messages which should act as a reference point for all communications. It provides a resource to develop content in your website and campaigns. This must not be a one-off exercise which is soon forgotten. It should be a constant source of reference to ensure your message does not slip back into simple features and benefits.

Your marketing must tell a much bigger story. This story portrays the real value you provide to customers. It explains why they should believe that you are the right choice to help them. Remember, they are only interested in their own desires, challenges, and problems.

8.

What are the marketing goals?

Now we are ready to put the plan together. There are four key components to every successful marketing plan: Objectives, Strategies, Tactics and Actions.

Objectives are the measurable goals. They always begin with the word "To".

Strategies define how you will achieve the measurable goals. They always begin with the word "By". They answer the question "How are we going to achieve the objective?".

Tactics are the specific marketing tools and activities which must be undertaken to fulfil each strategy.

Actions are the detailed steps and stages which are scheduled and measured to deliver the tactics required.

The marketing objectives should obviously tie in with the overall business objectives, so the marketing investment contributes measurably to the financial results.

In practise objectives, strategies, tactics, and actions exist at all levels in a business and cascade across functions. For example:

The Business Objective and Business Strategy
To achieve $10m of sales **by** entering a new market next year

The Marketing Objective and Marketing Strategy
To enter a new market next year **by** positioning product for specific persona

CASCADE NESTING

What are the marketing goals?

BUSINESS OBJECTIVE | BUSINESS STRATEGY | BUSINESS TACTICS

= MARKETING OBJECTIVE | MARKETING STRATEGY | MARKETING TACTICS

= MARKETING COMMUNICATIONS OBJECTIVE | MARKETING COMMUNICATIONS STRATEGY | MARKETING COMMUNICATIONS TACTICS

= SOCIAL MEDIA OBJECTIVE | SOCIAL MEDIA STRATEGY | SOCIAL MEDIA TACTICS

So, the best starting point to define marketing objectives is to look at the strategies set out in the business plan. If there is no business plan, or the strategic element is lacking, then marketers have to reverse-engineer to ensure that their objectives are fully aligned with the business goals.

Each marketing objective will have several strategies supporting it, each strategy will have a range of tactics and each tactic will have a myriad of actions scheduled overtime.

What are the marketing goals?

STRATEGY PYRAMID

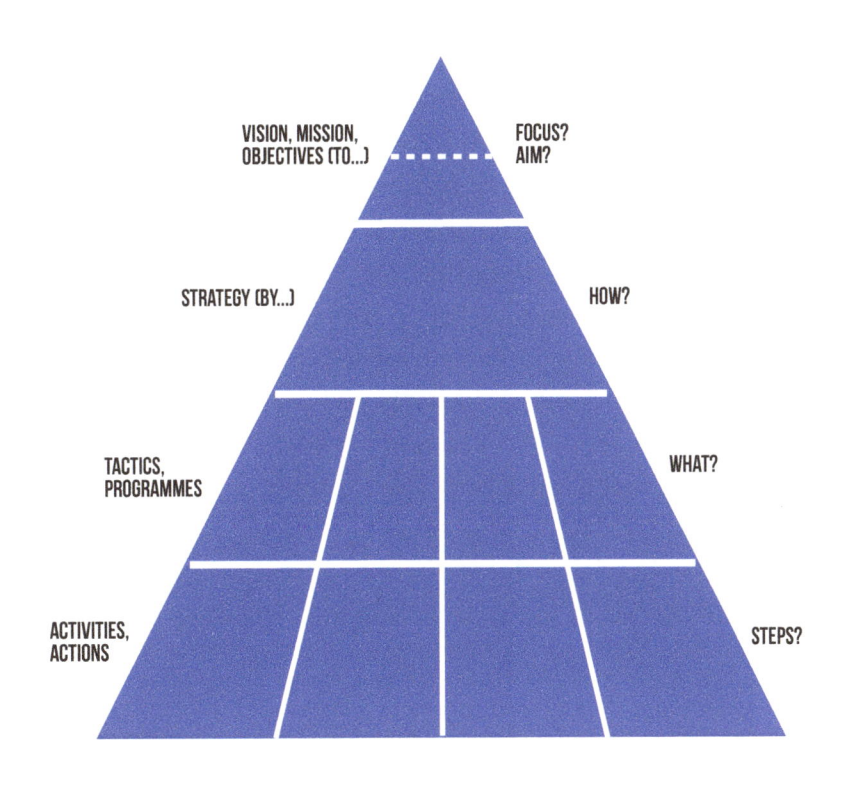

VISION, MISSION, OBJECTIVES (TO...) — FOCUS? AIM?

STRATEGY (BY...) — HOW?

TACTICS, PROGRAMMES — WHAT?

ACTIVITIES, ACTIONS — STEPS?

Lead Conversion Model

The most common requirement which is set as a marketing objective is to generate more sales leads or enquiries. However, before setting this as an objective, it is essential to understand the complete lead conversion model that runs right through the customer journey. It is frequently the case that businesses already have enough leads, but are failing to convert them as they progress along the journey. Most websites already have plenty of visitors. But they fail to provide those visitors with whatever they are looking for to move on to the next stage of their journey. Of course, it is possible that your marketing campaigns are simply attracting the wrong sort of leads, poor quality clicks or people finding you in error. Either way a marketing objective to increase the number of leads should be paired with a marketing objective to improve conversion rate as well. The largest cost comes from finding new leads, so it makes sense to look after the ones you have already got properly.

Please check that your lead process is working correctly on a regular basis. It is surprisingly common for new enquiries to end up in a junk folder, spam filter, an unmonitored email address or messages left are not returned. Automated workflows can get broken inadvertently or through the original architect moving on and no one knowing exactly how it all works.

If your potential customers first point of contact is through a lead management process which fails, they are unlikely to believe your product is of excellent quality. So, ensure that your lead process is fully documented and checked on a regular basis so that you never risk wasting and neglecting hard won enquiries.

The other common failure in lead generation, is to give up too soon. Campaigns are often abandoned after just a few emails or just a few days because instant results are not achieved. It has often been stated that it takes 7 points of contact to secure a sale, yet most sales people give up after 1 or 2. Some of the most successful lead generation email campaigns have as many as 30 different emails at different stages over several months. So, persistence and frequency are essential for success. (Tip: Don't be afraid of people unsubscribing - they were never going to buy from you anyway).

MoSoLo Objectives

One of the key objectives for many marketing teams is to retain and grow existing customers. Existing customers are already familiar with your service and are hopefully positive and enthusiastic about their relationship with the business, your products, and services. Positive customer equity provides a great foundation for future growth either through offering enhanced levels of service or additional products.

What could you do to encourage customers to:

Spend **mo**re

Come back **so**oner

Stay **lo**nger

Think about setting a marketing objective to increase average order value, or increase frequency of purchase, or extend the length of contact (even lifetime value) of a customer.

Be careful not to set too many objectives since by the time you layer in multiple strategies, each with their own sets of tactics and actions, it is very easy to build a plan which is impossible to deliver.

9.

How are you going to achieve the goals?

Marketing Strategies define how you will achieve the goals and objectives set out in the previous section. They always begin with the word "By".

So, for example a hotel might set a marketing objective **to** encourage guests to stay for 1 extra night. There are many ways **by** which this could be achieved:

    by offering the 3rd night at half price
    by making it feel like more like home
    by making guests aware of all the facilities
    by promoting special events

These are strategies – they show how the objective will be achieved.

Traditionally marketers have used lists of strategies beginning with the letter P, initially there were 4Ps, then 7 or 8:

Product, Place (distribution), Price, Promotion, People (customer service), Process (customer journey), Physical Evidence, Partners. etc.

These are useful headings as a "marketing mix" check list to help consider the key topics which your strategies could focus on. However, it is easy to end up with strategies that no longer align with the objectives and a tactical plan which is too big and complex to fulfil.

Whatever business you are in, it is likely that you have existing customers that you wish to retain. New customers that you wish to acquire. Lost customers that you would like to regain, and a small group of really loyal customers who could be your ambassadors.

So, start by defining your strategies in the following areas:

"Talking to Strangers" - New Customer Acquisition

"Friends and Family" - Existing Customer Relationship and Retention

"Raising the dead" - Regaining lost customers

"Loving your fans" - Generating referrals

Then consider strategies for each of the MoSoLo objectives:

>Spend **mo**re: – by increasing order value

>Come back **so**oner – by increasing frequency of purchase

>Stay **lo**nger: – by extending the length of the relationship

When you have finished listing your strategies double check to make sure that every one of them is aligned to one of the marketing objectives. Please avoid orphaned strategies as these may be little more them vanity projects.

Strategies are the essential link between objectives and tactics, they should ensure that all tactics have an impact on achieving the objectives.

10.

What are the specific activities and tasks?

Now taking each of the strategies in turn, run through the list of marketing tactics below. Build a complete list of all the possible tactics, tools and activities that could be deployed to deliver your strategy. It is important not to restrict your thinking at this stage - just generate the ideas and options. At a later stage you can decide which are feasible and affordable but for now let's keep the options open. Please note the 85 examples given below are just for guidance and are by no means a complete list.

Public Relations (PR)

Press releases, news updates, feature articles, interviews, comments, messaging, publicity events, speaking opportunities, blogs, social media, video, and audio news releases.

Content

Case studies, newsletters, sales collateral, awards, fact sheets, presentations, product toolkits, blogs, video, podcasts.

Digital & design

Website, landing pages, SEO, user experience, video, brand assets, graphic design, creative concepts, image library, automation, artificial intelligence, technologies, systems, apps.

Advertising

Online, (PPC, remarketing, banners) Offline (billboards, TV, radio, signage, magazines, trade press, door to door, inserts, point-of-sale).

Events

Stand design, collateral, publicity, invitations, promotions, sponsorship, webinars, conferences, social / entertainment, trade shows, concessions

Direct Marketing

Email, telemarketing, contact lists, mail, database, data quality.

What are the specific activities and tasks?

CRM

Customer journey, marketing automation, lead nurturing, lead scoring, conversion rate, customer data, data quality, workflows, personas, referrals.

Social Media

Tools & platforms, content, authoring, publishing, commenting, posting, promoting, social listening, communities.

Analysis & Insight

Website analytics, PPC & SEO performance, social media analytics, campaign reports, user analysis, behavioural analysis, transactional analysis, data analysis.

Channel & Partner

Support materials, content, presentations, tool kits, collaboration, promotions, offers.

Sales

Target hit list, call rate, conversion model, price, offers, support materials, key accounts, account-based marketing.

Product Management

Product range, new products, launches, promotions, R&D, testing, forecasting, suppliers.

You should now have an extensive list of tactics under each heading with a clear understanding of how each tactic will deliver on the strategies. It's important to balance the certainty of impact from established tactical activities with newer ideas where the outcome is more difficult to predict. Limitations on resources and budget may mean that prioritisation of tactics will be necessary.

Essential to waste 10% of your budget.

It is always the case that no matter how good or how successful your marketing tactic and campaign is today, one day it will fail. When that happens, you will need to develop a different approach and generate new ideas so that you continue to achieve the objectives. The problem comes if you do not already have the alternative ideas scoped out, developed, tested and on the shelf ready to go.

So, set aside 10% of your marketing budget to experiment, no return required, pure marketing R&D and testing. That way you are fully prepared for the day when leads suddenly drop off a cliff. (Tip: Always be testing.)

11.

How are you going to schedule and ensure delivery?

To manage the marketing plan, we now need to turn these tactics into actions and time specific schedules.

Key Action and Initiatives Schedule

The simplest approach is to define the date for each tactical activity across each of the four quarters in the year. Laying these out in a table will show very quickly if the volume of activity is too great in any quarter of the year. Typically, quarter one always seems to be the busiest. So, scheduling across the whole year will ensure that marketing activity and campaigns are sustained and in line with resources available. There will be some activities such as social media where the activity is constant and therefore it is tempting to log it as simply "ongoing". Please avoid this so that you are specifying different stages and phases throughout the year.

Having set out the list of marketing tactic activities for each quarter of the year, it's time to draw the costs together to produce the marketing budget. A quick reference back to the objectives will show if this budget is viable. Remember that marketing expenditure is an investment which must deliver commercial results.

Once you are happy that the quarterly plans will deliver the required results, they should be converted into a month-by-month plan (Marketing Calendar) so that activity begins to be defined to a more detailed level.

Action Plan

Now take each of your strategies and develop a detailed action plan table which breaks down each of the tactics into specific tasks. Each task should link to the objective and strategy it supports (the "What" and "How") and then have the following elements:

Deadline date (When?)
Measure of success (How much?)
Name of person responsible (Who?)
Status (Progress?)

How are you going to schedule and ensure delivery?

ACTION PLAN TEMPLATE

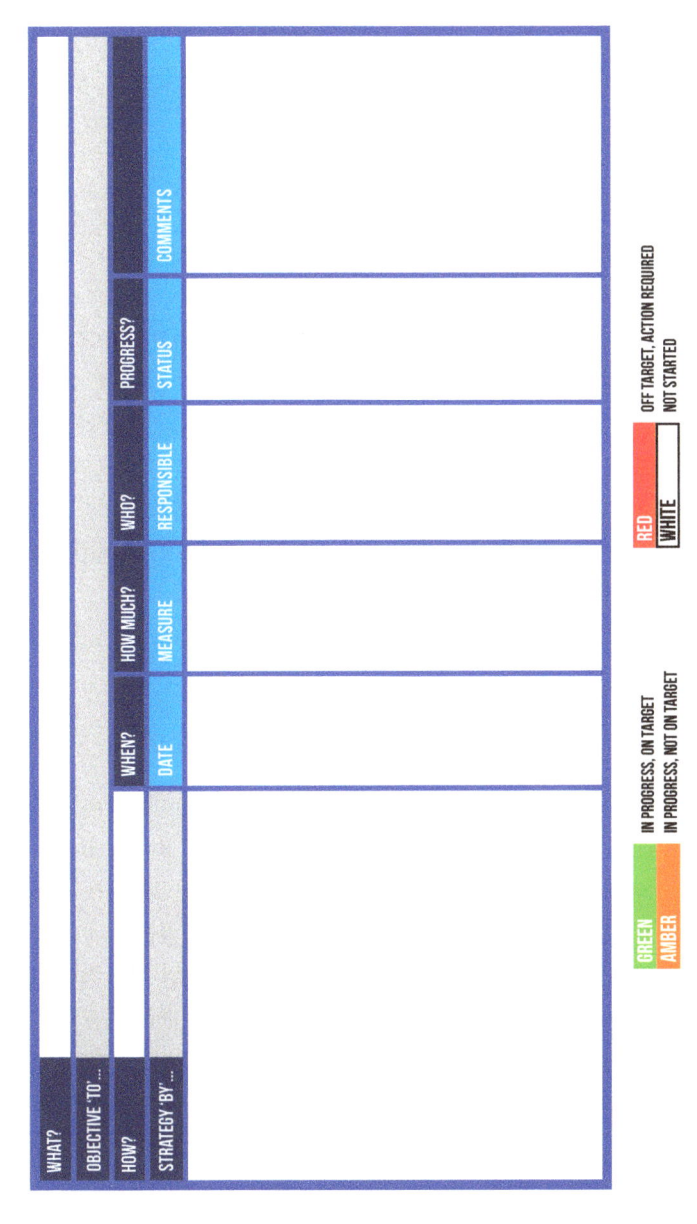

WHAT?	OBJECTIVE TO:...	HOW?	STRATEGY BY:...
WHEN? DATE	HOW MUCH? MEASURE	WHO? RESPONSIBLE	PROGRESS? STATUS	COMMENTS

GREEN IN PROGRESS, ON TARGET
AMBER IN PROGRESS, NOT ON TARGET
RED OFF TARGET, ACTION REQUIRED
WHITE NOT STARTED

All these plans should be visible and shared openly so the entire organisation is aware and able to contribute or support as necessary.

Project management

For longer and more complex initiatives a full project management process should be considered using one of the many project management tools or spreadsheet templates. Breaking projects down into 90-day sprints helps ensure that progress is maintained, and key barriers are identified early and resolved. Visibility and reporting across the organisation are essential with major long-term projects.

Briefing and Managing an Agency

It is unlikely that you will have all skills, knowledge, and resource that you need within the business to fulfil all marketing activity successfully. There are specialist areas like design, brand, TV, or video where it may not be feasible to hold the necessary skills in house and where an external agency would be able to leverage wider experience and skills. Content creation, social media, PR, and digital marketing are also frequently outsourced to specialist marketing agencies.

So why do these relationships so often go wrong?

How are you going to schedule and ensure delivery?

There are two main reasons: firstly, keeping the agency at arm's length or regarding them as a supplier rather than a partner. Secondly, not producing a written brief and plan which sets out the requirements clearly.

Successfully outsourcing marketing activity to a third party can only be achieved if you regard them as being as much part of your team as someone who is employed by the business. Therefore, they should have the same level of access to information, plans, news, and updates as if they were full time employees – they are just paid differently. Do not forget that you will need to motivate the outsourced team too - not just dump tasks on them. (Tip: to get the best from your agency partners be the client that they all want to work with and give them the opportunity to do their best work)

Talk to any marketing agency director and they will tell you that they very rarely receive an adequate brief from the client. As a result, a lot of time and effort is wasted trying to establish the requirements or heading off in the wrong direction. The secret to achieving outstanding results with outsourced marketing agencies is to write a clear succinct written brief. This explains what it is you want to achieve, what you want done, how you will measure success, and how much you want to spend. To ensure clarity, the brief should always be in writing, not verbal. Always share the full marketing plan (Chapter 13) and brand messaging guidelines (Chapter 7).

Key headings might include:

Background, Marketing Objectives, Sales Objectives, Branding, Lessons from previous marketing, Communications Objectives, Target Audience & Insights, Key Message/Proposition, Emotional and Functional Benefits, What will Customers Think or Do, Tone of Voice, Brand Personality, Timings/Key Dates, Budget, Success Criteria, Mandatory Guidelines, Approvals Process.

No sign off marketing - draining the approval swamp

This may seem a bit radical. The most common status of all marketing tasks is "waiting for approval" whether it's your agencies or your own team. This 100% guarantees slow speed when you need to go fast, and drains out energy, pride, passion, and drive.

So, remove all checks, supervision, and approvals. From now on, whoever creates it, is 100% responsible for it. No safety net. It is their name on it after all, so they have a clear need to get it right before they hit send. Too often marketers and agencies no longer own their work once it has been mauled, sanitised, and delayed through a multi-layer approval process. If you know your work is going to be checked several times, why bother trying to make it perfect? If you know your ideas or designs are going to be changed anyway, why bother refining them or making them your best?

Every time, I have persuaded clients to remove approvals, marketing productivity, output, and team motivation have risen massively. Guess what? The results have improved too.

You cannot hold your marketing teams or agencies to account for their results if the reality is that other people have modified and delayed everything. Empowered and trusted teams always produce better results.

If of course they wish to seek some guidance, that's fine, but let them own it 100% and be grateful for your input.

If you still insist on sign off (maybe for regulatory or legal purposes), then at least put in place a default approval process. The assumption is that everything is approved by default after 24 hours unless notified to the contrary. The most critical success factor in all marketing is getting stuff out of the door.

Lead qualification, scoring and nurturing

All leads and enquiries are not equal. Some may be very early in their customer journey and just researching, (typically 90% of first-time website visitors are not planning to make a purchase), others just may not be quite the right fit. So, in managing the lead pipeline it is important to qualify and score leads so they can be treated in the most effective manner.

Lead scoring assesses a customer lead based on their level of engagement with the company or product and how well they match the target persona that the business knows it can serve well. For example, someone who spends a lot of time looking at your website, watches your videos, signs up to your webinars and downloads your content would score highly for level of engagement with business. If they also closely matched your ideal persona, they are probably worth a phone call! Similarly, if someone who closely matched your ideal persona visited your website but engaged no further, you would wish to instigate actions to nurture their interest and engagement.

There are many marketing automation platforms which can automate the scoring and nurturing process. Prospects therefore receive appropriate levels of marketing intervention to draw them along their journey without the need for manual activity. As always software is not the solution to marketing problems, it's the thinking that must be done first. The hardest part of marketing automation is not in learning to use the software platform. The challenge is in thinking through and mapping out the stages of the customer journey and creating the library of marketing assets for each stage and each eventuality.

Every lead that enters your CRM system needs to be qualified. Marketing automation systems may automatically bring useful qualification data, but it may still need a manual process to establish what you really need to know.

How are you going to schedule and ensure delivery?

For example: a typical B2B lead qualification checklist for a telephone follow up following a website enquiry:

LEAD QUALIFICATION CHECKLIST

1. COMPANY DETAILS?
2. HOW DO YOU KNOW ABOUT US?
3. REQUIREMENTS / NEEDS?
4. BUDGET?
5. JOB TITLE/ROLE AND APPROVAL PROCESS?
6. WHAT IS THE CONTEXT / BIGGER PICTURE?
7. COMPETITORS?
8. EXISTING SERVICES, SUPPLIERS AND COSTS?
9. TIMESCALE / DEADLINES?
10. IMPACT ON THE BUSINESS & PERSON IF NOT PROGRESSED?

12.

How are you going to measure results?

One of the great benefits of modern marketing is that we have phenomenal ability to measure and analyse campaigns and activities. Today, we really can understand what's working and what's not working. With highly complex analytics tools, sophisticated dashboards and statistical analysis sitting behind every digital platform there is the risk of getting lost in the analysis. The problem is that we have too much data which leads to all analysis and no action. Further, it is too easy to adopt simplistic metrics without the depth of interpretation necessary and make the wrong decision.

Monitoring and Analytics

The sheer complexity of performance data available to us deters many from using it to best advantage. It is surprising how many organisations do not use the basic analytics tools freely available to them. Instead, they rely on "trust and hope" that their marketing is going to work. Just giving everyone a login to access the dashboard or analytics tools is not a solution either. There is no alternative but to invest the time and effort to understand the analysis tools available to you. To take the time to interpret what that data is telling you and define actions as a result. Mastery of the tools is a fundamental requirement for all modern marketers. Whilst you may outsource certain activities to specialist agencies, you still must fully understand what it is you are outsourcing. How will you measure success and how will you refocus, or redirect efforts as required?

(Tip: set the rule "No reports without narrative, No analysis without actions".)

Conversion Rate

At every stage of the customer journey or sales funnel there should be accurate measurement to monitor the conversion rate. So, for example if your website has an enquiry form it is crucial to measure how many visitors complete the form. As well as, what they look at on their way and the point at which they abandon. Measuring this allows you to constantly adjust the site layout and content to improve the number of visitors who complete your goal by making an enquiry.

(Tip: use Heat Map tools to show you exactly where visitors click on the site.)

Multi-channel and Attribution

If you have mapped out your customer journey fully and used the full depth of the analytics tools available, you will appreciate the complex and random nature of customer behaviour. Your customers will be engaging with your business or product through many different channels sometimes at the same time. It is often difficult to appreciate the logic of these behaviours but simply recognising that they exist is sufficient. An enquiry might be received through your website, but the critical question is: what was it that encouraged the prospective customer to visit your website in the first place? This is usually a complex web of social and media channels, content, and influences. Therefore, it is essential to measure all the channels that contribute to the customer enquiry, not just the one where they completed the form. Conversion is normally assisted by other parts of your marketing programme and therefore correct attribution of their roles are essential.

It is enlightening to realise that the enquiry that came through your Facebook page originally searched on Google, heard your radio advertisement, visited your website, saw your remarketed adverts, checked reviews, opened your 5th email, then whilst on Facebook clicked on your advert to enquire. If you did not know all this, the chances are that you would place all your budget on Facebook. Remember the customer journey - the point at which a prospect converts is not the totality of their journey or relationship with your brand. Just measuring the lead source is not sufficient.

(Tip: customers don't always tell you the truth when you ask them how they heard of you.)

Key Marketing Performance Indicators

The ideal is that every role or team should be focussed on the core levers which drive a business like some efficient well-oiled machine with everyone working on their key drivers.

Whilst business leaders love KPIs, their teams are often less enamoured to the extent that KPIs often cause lower performance. They see no benefit to them just more admin, reporting, pressure, and hassle. In some organisations, marketers spend more than half their time creating reports, so have little scope to do any marketing!

Part of the problem is that data availability is now so easy with personal dashboards and analytics tools you can drown in it without too much effort.

So, to achieve genuine performance improvement, Key Marketing Performance Indicators should exist at different levels:

Activity level (self-measure)

These are day to day parameters which an individual will use to manage their own focus, priority, and performance. They have no direct impact on others. They do not need to be reported on. Management should only be interested in confirming that individuals are setting their own Activity Measures, measuring their own success, and adjusting activity accordingly.

Impact level (lead measure)

These are the tangible impacts or effects of the individual activities above. They may have impact on others. Management should be aware of these and be interested in these measures.

Output level (lag measure)

These are the key business drivers. They are the desired output, effect, and outcome of activities. Management should be fully aware of these and seeking improvement at every opportunity.

Process level (ratios)

These are performance ratios that record stages in processes. They may exist within a team or between teams. They are ideal for real time dashboards, so long as they tie into actions (corrective or celebratory).

Finance level (ratios)

These are largely backward looking and measure key financial trends. They should also be projected forward into forecasts to alert to risk and exposure.

Conversion Model (Ratio)

These are the activity or action steps leading to gaining a new customer, regaining a lapsed customer, or securing a repeat customer. The conversion model shows how a prospective customer progresses along the journey or sales funnel and defines how many contacts are required based on the conversion at each stage. e.g.

100 Contacts : 50 Leads : 10 Opportunities : 1 Client

So, in this scenario, if you start with 100 cold contacts, 50% convert to leads (i.e. have some level of need and interest), of these 20% (10) progress to Opportunity level (i.e. defined budget and timescale, quotation sent) with 10% (1) becoming a client.

(Tip: Remember the 2 basic ways to increase revenue: Improve conversion rate at each stage and Increase number of cold contacts.)

Examples of Marketing KPIs:

1 Key Activity Indicator (Self)
Social Media Posts per channel (tweets, updates, blog etc.), shares / likes
Emails sent
Outbound phone calls
Data records cleaned
Content published
Fixes and adjustments to campaigns
Adverts run / boosted

How are you going to measure results?

2 Key Impact Indicator (Outcome)
Downloads
Website analytics (visitors, engagement level, source etc.)
Registrations, Conversions, Responses
Enquiries / leads (number and £ value)
Database growth, Data completion%
Opportunities (number & £ value)

3 Key Output Indicator (Key Busines Drivers)
Proposals sent (number and £ value)
Quotations (number and £ value)
Orders (number and £ value)
Lost projects (number and £ value)
Repeat projects (number and £ value)
Client growth (number and £ value)
Project size growth (number and £ value)

4 Key Finance Indicator
Sales (Revenue, orders, pipeline, discount)
Profit (service, client)
Product (profit per product)
Employee (profit, sales, discount)
Customer (profit, revenue, debtor days)
Finance (capital, stock, cash, assets)
HR (absence, recruitment, productivity)

5 Conversion Ratio Model
For each of the following, number, and value (£):

Existing Clients
Hot contact : Leads : Opportunity : Repeat Client

Lapsed Clients
Warm / Cool contact : Leads : Opportunity : Regained Client

New Clients
Cold contact: Leads : Opportunity : New Client

Flash Reports

The sheer complexity of modern marketing makes it difficult to keep track of all initiatives and activities at the right level. There is a temptation to have regular update meetings and reports. But this wastes scarce time and contributes little to the motivation of the marketing team. There can never be any benefit in holding a marketing meeting in which people simply report on their activity. The easiest solution is for every member of the team to send a brief "news flash" email update every Friday afternoon to everyone.

The Flash Report has 3 sections (bullet points only):

a) Progress and Achievements for the current week.
This ensures that actions from the previous week are implemented and provides everyone with insight on the scale and level of activity of others in the team.

b) Priorities and Actions planned for next week.
This provides insight into next week's workload and potential pressure points and means that everyone starts the next week with a plan.

c) Urgent, Specific and Critical Issues
These are areas where help, guidance and support are required.

Then on Monday mornings, everyone can talk through their update, adding colour and context so that understanding is developed, assistance sought, and thinking is progressed. This leads to quality discussion and action rather than just reporting. You may even find that the reports tell you all you need to know, so a team meeting is not necessary!

13.

What's in the plan?

Marketing plans have traditionally included much insight and analysis; marketers sometimes see this as the prime purpose of the marketing plan. As we've explored in this book, a thorough understanding of the market opportunities, your customer personas, and the brand messages is fundamental to developing the marketing plan. However, the plan itself should focus entirely on action - on what you are going to do to achieve the goal. Therefore, all the good work on insight and analysis should be relegated to the appendix to avoid cluttering up a commercially focused marketing plan. The marketing plan should define what you going to do, not the logic and rationale for doing it. Action not analysis.

Marketing Plan Summary

1. Situational Analysis
    Market Opportunities
    Market Threats
    Business Strengths
    Business Weaknesses

2. Key Issues
    Conclusions from the situational analysis

3. Objectives
    The objective is what you want to achieve
    (always begins with the word "To" and has a quantifiable measure)

4. Strategy
    The strategy is how you are going to achieve that objective
    (always begins with the word "by"

5. Tactics
    The Tactics are the specific tools and activities which must be undertaken to fulfil each strategy

PR
(e.g. press releases, features, interviews, comments, messaging)

What's in the plan?

Content
(e.g. case studies, sales collateral, awards, fact sheets, presentations, product toolkits)

Digital & design
(e.g. website, SEO, PPC, UX, video, brand, assets)

Advertising
(e.g. online, offline)

Events
(stand design, collateral, publicity, invitations, promotions)

Direct Marketing
(e.g. email, telemarketing, lists, mail)

CRM
(e.g. customer journey, automation, lead nurturing, conversion, data quality, personas)

Social Media
(e.g. social listening, tools & platforms, content)

Analysis & Insight
(e.g. web analytics, PPC & SEO performance)

Channel & Partner
(e.g. support materials, content)

Sales
(e.g. target hit list, call rate, conversion model, price, offers)

Product Management
(e.g. product range, new products, launches, promotions, R&D, testing, forecasting, suppliers)

6. Key Actions & Initiatives

Schedule of what is going to happen.
Q1
Q2
Q3
Q4

7. Action Plan

Detailed schedule of what is going to happen, when (by week) and cost.

8. Appendix

Product history
Problems solved / needs satisfied
Customer Journey, personas, insight, and analysis
Market insight and analysis
Competitive frame & positioning
Purpose and principles
Business Model
Value Proposition
Brand values and messaging
Any other supporting information for reference.

The Marketing Plan Process

Having now drafted your action focussed marketing plan with a range of activities scheduled to deliver your objectives here is a summary of the overall process. This shows the key stages and the outcomes from each.

Inevitably not every tactic will deliver the results you intended, so please do not neglect the need to constantly revisit, learn and revise your approach.

"The Business Leaders Essential Guide to Marketing"

MARKETING PLAN PROCESS

ASSESS

- ASSESS AND UNDERSTAND SITUATION (WHO DOES IT?)
- AUDIT (WHO DOES IT?) — KNOWLEDGE & GAPS CONFIRMED
- SITUATION ANALYSIS (WHO DOES IT?) — OPPORTUNITIES/ISSUES AGREED
- CUSTOMER INSIGHT (WHO DOES IT?) — TARGET CUSTOMER FOCUS AGREED

FOCUS

- REFOCUS BUSINESS MODEL (WHO DOES IT?) — ALIGNED TO CUSTOMER FOCUS
- BRAND AND MESSAGING (WHO DOES IT?) — RESONATES WITH TARGET PERSONAS
- 3 YEAR AIMS, GOALS & OBJECTIVES (WHO DOES IT?) — SCALE OF MARKETING TASK AGREED

ACTION

- MARKETING PRIORITY PLANS (STRATEGY) (WHO DOES IT?) — PRIORITY FOCUS PUBLISHED
- MARKETING PLAN (NEW CUSTOMER ACQUISITION) (WHO DOES IT?) — SPECIFIC ACTIVITIES SCHEDULED
- LEAD MANAGEMENT & CONVERSION (WHO DOES IT?) — GOALS ACHIEVED OR PLAN REVISED
- RETENTION PLAN (WHO DOES IT?) — SPECIFIC ACTIVITIES SCHEDULED
- RENEWALS AND REFERRALS (WHO DOES IT?) — RETAIN & GROW EXISITING CUSTOMERS

14.

What might go wrong?

Lead volumes too high or too low
Too many leads? – always wise to test and roll out a campaign gradually.
Too few leads? – time for a rethink of approach or budget.
"Keep your sales pipeline full by prospecting continuously. Always have more people to see than you have time to see them." Brian Tracy

Lead conversion too low
Not converting leads successfully and gifting them to competitors. Are these just the wrong sort of leads or is your conversion process failing?
"Your future prospects resemble your best customers, and that's the place you should start." Holger Schulze

Not on top of the marketing technology tools
If you do not have mastery of your tools, you cannot manage others to do it.
"Mastery is great, but even that is not enough. You have to be able to change course without a bead of sweat, or remorse." Tom Peters

Simplistic analysis and assumption
Assuming the lead source is the whole story – the lead occurs through a complex array of influences, actions, and impressions.

Sales v marketing conflict
"Sales and marketing alignment is about one shared goal: revenue that is delivered or over-delivered every quarter. There will always be tension, but that tension can be positive if there is a culture of clear expectations and communication." Craig Rosenberg

No social media hamster wheel
Regular posting is essential to maintain visibility, otherwise its "out of sight, out of mind".
"We don't have a choice on whether we do social media, the question is how well we do it." Erik Qualman

Competitors competing for clicks
Sometimes competitors seem to throw excessive money to secure clicks – should your response be fight or flight? Larger competitors with deep pockets may not monitor their marketing performance closely, so they frequently overspend in ignorance.

"The competitor to be feared is one who never bothers about you at all but goes on making his own business better all the time." Henry Ford

Targeting everyone
Trying to appeal to everyone ensures you appeal to no one. No focus leads to bland marketing. A narrow niche focus makes everything easier and more effective.
"In marketing I've seen only one strategy that can't miss - and that is to market to your best customers first, your best prospects second and the rest of the world last." John Romero

Internal marketing
Make sure everyone knows what is happening, so they can help. "Internal marketing is probably much more important than external marketing". Tom Stewart

Inbound only
Publishing lots of relevant content and allowing customers to sell to themselves is ideal. But outbound activity is also essential to reach new customers too.

Content creation – quality and quantity
Must be a constant activity and not held up by the approval process. "Either write something worth reading or do something worth writing about." Benjamin Franklin

"Content is king." Bill Gates

"Good content isn't about good storytelling. It's about telling a true story well." Ann Handley

Expecting instant results and giving up too soon
Customers work at their own pace, not yours. They do not see most of what you send them or are too busy with something else. Marketing is a long game which requires persistence and frequency.
"The man who stops advertising to save money is like the man who stops the clock to save time." Thomas Jefferson

Not testing
The market knows best what works.
It costs nothing to test properly.
"The one size fits all approach of standardised testing is convenient but lazy." James Dyson

Build it and they will come
Why should they? How do they become aware?
Why would they admit their previous purchase was wrong?
Even the best products do not sell themselves.
"Build it, and they will come" only works in the movies. Social Media is a "build it, nurture it, engage them and they may come and stay." Seth Godin

"Marketing is no longer about the stuff you make, but about the stories you tell." Seth Godin

Not completing the loop

Feeding back campaign results into a learning cycle of what works or does not and why.

"I think it's very important to have a feedback loop, where you're constantly thinking about what you've done and how you could be doing it better." Elon Musk

All analysis, no action

"Analysis creates paralysis. You can't be 100 percent sure of anything." Mark Burnett

Too much reliance on research

"The trouble with market research is that people don't think what they feel, they don't say what they think, and they don't do what they say." David Ogilvy

Forgetting it's all about the customer

"The aim of marketing is to know and understand the customer so well the product or service fits him and sells itself." Peter Drucker,

"Advertising works most effectively when it's in line with what people are already trying to do." Mark Zuckerberg

"People spend money when and where they feel good." Walt Disney

"If people believe they share values with a company, they will stay loyal to the brand." Howard Schultz

Standing Still
"Marketing's job is never done. It's about perpetual motion. We must continue to innovate every day." Beth Comstock

The Four Failures
"No one noticed it.
People noticed it but decided they didn't want to try it.
People tried it but decided not to keep using it.
People liked it but didn't tell their friends." Seth Godin

15.

Recommended Reading

The Business Leaders Essential Guide to Growth
Stephen Dann

The Business Leaders Essential Guide to Innovation
Stephen Dann

Value Proposition Design
Alexander Osterwalder, Ives Pigneur, Greg Bernarda, and Alan Smith

The Ultimate Question
Frederick Reichheld

Alchemy. The surprising power of ideas that don't make sense
Rory Sutherland

All Marketers Are Liars
Seth Godin

This is Marketing
Seth Godin

Marketing Plans: How to prepare them, how to profit from them
Malcolm McDonald, and Hugh Wilson

Positioning
Al Ries and Jack Trout

Crossing the Chasm
Geoffrey A Moore

Briefing an Agency best practice guide
IPA

Your Ad Ignored Here
Tom Fishburne (Marketoonist)

The Choice Factory
Richard Shotton

About the Author

Stephen Dann is a creative thinker, innovator, marketer, strategist, author, and renowned business adviser.

He has built and led marketing teams in 5 major organisations building high performing teams, harnessing new technology and innovative approaches. Leaving corporate life behind, he developed a series of small and medium sized enterprises and fully experienced the highs and lows of the entrepreneurial journey.

He founded Business Impact Solutions Ltd in 2005 specifically to help business leaders and entrepreneurs tackle the challenges of growth, marketing, and innovation. As a business, management, and marketing consultant he has worked with over 400 client companies to date, ranging from mature global corporates and not for profit organisations to SMEs and high growth early-stage businesses across a wide range of sectors. He is a registered expert for the European Commission and is regularly called on to advise on the commercialisation of ground-breaking innovation.

Stephen is passionate about innovation, creativity, and change. He is recognised for seeking new ideas and insights to help businesses solve their commercial problems through creative and imaginative use of technology and marketing.

He believes that organisations only truly fulfil their potential and achieve their goals if they change the way they behave, change the way they operate or change some other fundamental aspect of the business. He constantly reminds business leaders that doing what you have always done and just exhorting teams to work harder is the best way to ensure those goals are not achieved.

Stephen is dedicated to helping businesses fix the problems that prevent organisations, teams, and individuals from achieving their potential.

As a sought-after business coach, consultant, and speaker, Stephen openly shares his tried, tested, and innovative approaches with entrepreneurs, business leaders and their teams.

Information on Stephen's books, insights and other materials can be found at:

www.businessimpactsolutions.co.uk

Lightning Source UK Ltd.
Milton Keynes UK
UKHW020719150522
403018UK00001B/3